D0561023

NORTHERN H. S. LIBRARY

The
Dream
Long
Deferred

The
Dream
Long
Deferred

NORTHERN H. S. LIBRARY

Frye Gaillard

DREAM LONG DEFERRED   11009
GAILLARD FRYE   370.19GA

The University of North Carolina Press

Chapel Hill & London

© 1988 Frye Gaillard

All rights reserved

Manufactured in the United States of America

Library of Congress Cataloging-in-Publication Data

Gaillard, Frye, 1946–

  The dream long deferred.

  Includes index.

  1. Busing for school integration—North Carolina—
Charlotte—History. 2. School integration—North
Carolina—Charlotte—History. I. Title.

LC214.523.C48G35 1988   370.19′342   87-35845

ISBN 0-8078-1794-5 (alk. paper)

ISBN 0-8078-4223-0 (pbk.: alk. paper)

The paper in this book meets the guidelines for
permanence and durability of the Committee on
Production Guidelines for Book Longevity of the
Council on Library Resources.

92 91 90 89 88 5 4 3 2 1

Frontispiece:
Dorothy Counts approaching Harding High
School, September 4, 1957
Photo credit: Don Sturkey, *The Charlotte Observer*

For Dorothy Counts, Julius Chambers,

James B. McMillan, William E. Poe,

Maggie Ray, and all the other

brave people of Charlotte

What happens to a dream deferred?

Langston Hughes

Contents

Acknowledgments

When I came to the Charlotte *Observer* in the early 1970s, my first real assignment was to cover the busing crisis of the local public schools—a national test case that, in profound and subtle ways, was reshaping the life of the city where it started. From the beginning, I was struck by the drama of the story, and for years I have wanted to go back and chronicle those events I had covered in the superficial rush (inevitable, I'm afraid) of daily journalism.

In 1985 and 1986, I finally got the chance, thanks in large measure to the financial support of the Z. Smith Reynolds Foundation, in cooperation with Queens College. I am grateful to those who made that support possible, especially Tom Lambeth, Billy Wireman, Dan Clodfelter, and Dennis and Betty Chafin Rash, all of whom believed in the importance of the story.

For help in the writing of it, I am indebted to many people and institutions. My Charlotte *Observer* colleagues Elizabeth Leland, Polly Paddock, Lisa Hammersly, and Ed Williams offered important criticism and support. Friends from other places and professions—Katherine Frye, Elizabeth Minnich, Garrett Epps, John Egerton, and my daughters, Rachel and Tracy Gaillard, both students in the Charlotte-Mecklenburg schools—offered needed feedback and encouragement at critical junctures. The fine staff of the special collections at the library of the University of North Carolina at Charlotte guided me through the papers of Julius Chambers and Ben Horack, and the rulings of Judge James B. McMillan; and the files of the Charlotte *Observer* and the Charlotte *News* demonstrated the historical importance of good newspapers. Maggie Ray, Betsy Bennett, William Waggoner, and Eleanor Brawley, participants in the controversy, made their personal files available, and many dozens of others agreed to lengthy interviews. School officials, especially former Superintendent Jay Robinson and his deputy Chris

Folk, a man of rare generosity and competence, made certain that I had whatever I needed.

I also relied on the writings of others: Richard Kluger's *Simple Justice*, the definitive account of the 1954 *Brown* decision; J. Anthony Lukas's *Common Ground*, which tells the very different story of Boston's experience with busing; *Swann's Way* by Bernard Schwartz and *The Brethren* by Bob Woodward and Scott Armstrong, both of which offer important accounts of the Supreme Court's consideration of the Charlotte case; and a doctoral dissertation by Howard Maniloff, a former education writer at the Charlotte *Observer* who became a respected educator in the Charlotte-Mecklenburg system.

In addition, I want to say special thanks to Nancy Frederick of the Charlotte-Mecklenburg schools, a teacher whose excellence, thankfully, was not an aberration during the period of time described in this book. She was not only my best and most reliable editor, but a friend whose support is literally irreplaceable.

I am grateful to all of these people. But I am most grateful to the people of Charlotte, whose triumph is worthy of any writer's best. They have grappled honestly and well with the American Dilemma, and have set—at least for a while—an example for the nation that deserves to be remembered.

Introduction

On October 8, 1984, President Ronald Reagan, then running for reelection, made a campaign stop in Charlotte, North Carolina. It was a clear autumn day, full of bright sunshine and American flags and, as was usually the case with Mr. Reagan's appearances, an enthusiastic crowd that cheered his words. But there was one moment that was unexpectedly awkward. Midway in his speech, the president departed from his standard campaign delivery to criticize Democrats for their support of "busing that takes innocent children out of the neighborhood school and makes them pawns in a social experiment that nobody wants. And we've found out that it failed."

It must have surprised the president, as he smiled out across the sea of white faces, that in contrast to nearly everything else he said, his denunciations of busing were greeted with silence: uncomfortable, embarrassed, almost stony. What could be the reason? Charlotte, after all, was the national test case for busing, and the experiment had begun in rocky fashion, with boycotts and white flight and violence day after day in the schools.

What Mr. Reagan seemed not to know, however, was that those upheavals had long since disappeared, replaced by more than a decade of intense community pride over the success of integration. As the Charlotte *Observer* put it in an adamant editorial entitled "You Were Wrong, Mr. President":

> Charlotte-Mecklenburg's proudest achievement of the past 20 years is not the city's impressive new skyline or its strong, growing economy. Its proudest achievement is its fully integrated school system. That system was born out of bitter controversy over court-ordered busing. It was shaped by caring citizens who refused to see their schools and their community torn apart by racial conflict. It was nourished by courageous elected officials,

creative school administrators and dedicated teachers and parents. It has blossomed into one of the nation's finest, recognized through the United States for quality, innovation and, most of all, for overcoming the most difficult challenge American public education has ever faced.

The editorial was reprinted in the Washington *Post*, but for the most part, outside of Charlotte, Mr. Reagan's faux pas was dismissed or unnoticed. Indeed, the president was not alone in his view of busing as an experiment that failed. With the dismal headlines from Boston, Norfolk, and other American cities, it has become almost an article of faith among liberals and conservatives alike that busing has been a tragedy. The purpose of this book is to make a simple point: whatever the experience of other cities, busing was not a tragedy in Charlotte. The inescapable truth of this city's experience is that by almost any measure you care to apply, busing succeeded in the first place it was tried. It strengthened the public schools, improved the racial climate, and ushered in a more effective and democratic era in the history of the local government. This is the story of how that happened. It is a human story, full of the drama that often goes with fierce determination and lofty aspiration; but in many ways, it is not really an extraordinary story. Many of the characters are unlikely heroes—people, black and white, who simply did not want to see their public schools destroyed or their city torn apart.

The drama began, you could argue, in early September of 1957, when Darius Swann, then an American missionary to India, picked up an English-language newspaper and found himself staring at the image on the cover: a picture of a young black girl in a prim checkered dress, a large bow at the collar, her head erect and defiant in her eye, but her face nearly stoic as she made her way through a mob. The power of the image struck Swann at once, for the photograph was large and vivid, and it was a shock to see it in Allahabad, India, a city of 500,000 near the Ganges River, half a world away from the United States.

Swann began to read the story and the caption beneath the picture, and he discovered that the girl was Dorothy Counts, the daughter of a longtime family friend. Swann found his mind roaming back to the days in Amelia County, Virginia, when he was the youngest of ten children in a black farm family and Dorothy's father, Herman Counts, was a kind of circuit-riding Presbyterian, a minister who presided at several churches in the area. Later, in Charlotte, Herman Counts had become a professor of philosophy at Johnson C. Smith University, and Darius soon followed him there as a student. After he graduated in 1948, now a minister himself, Swann accepted a call as a Presbyterian missionary—only the second black man to hold such a position in the twentieth century and the first outside the continent of Africa.

When Darius and his young wife Vera arrived at the port of Bombay, on January 1, 1953, Dorothy Counts was still a little girl. But nearly five years later, in September of 1957, she was fifteen years old and a high school sophomore, and because of her maturity and poise and her academic aptitude, she had been chosen as a Charlotte pioneer—one of four black students to break the color barrier in the local public schools.

The white students at Harding High School responded with hostility, and looking at the newspaper picture, the Swanns were startled at the cocky hatred in the faces. They had no way of knowing, of course, that seven years later they would return to Charlotte and help finish the job that Dorothy Counts was beginning. They would file a lawsuit against the Charlotte public schools, and a little more than four years after that, *Swann* v. *Charlotte-Mecklenburg* would become the national test case for busing and the instrument by which the city of Charlotte would emerge as a national model of constructive race relations. All of those events were well hidden in the future, and Darius and Vera Swann simply knew, as they stared at the newspaper in 1957, that the image on the page seemed fundamentally wrong. Their perceptions of the world had changed a great deal during their short time in India. These were the years after Gandhi's revolution, and they could still feel the spirit of it in the streets of Allahabad.

The Swanns did not make the tactical connection right away between Gandhi's nonviolent resistance to the British rule of India and what might be possible for the black movement at home. Only later, in 1955, when they began reading *Time* magazine's account of the Montgomery bus boycott, did they begin to see the promise of Gandhi's methods for America. But they made the leap immediately from Gandhi's powerful defense of Indian outcasts—his frequent use of the Hindi word *Harijan*, "the people of God," to describe the people at the bottom of the Indian social system. It stirred their imaginations to consider a similar vision for their native South.

In addition, the Swanns lived in India as the only blacks in a community of missionaries, relating to whites as people, not oppressors, for the first time in their lives. Indeed, until the beginning of their tenure in Allahabad, white people of decency, of a humanity untainted by condescension or cruelty, seemed to have existed only in legend. Now, however, things were very different among their fellow missionaries, and the Swanns discovered something basic about their own view of race relations. They had come to presume that whites were afflicted with some generic moral defect—some character flaw that pervaded a whole race of people and led its members naturally in the direction of oppression. But with a different experience in India, it began to occur to them that this might not be true and that whites, if removed from the system, the institution, the old habits of racism, might be capable of humanity after all.

In addition to all of that, the Swanns had begun to raise a family, and their two young children had never experienced racism, quite literally had lived in such a way that all its emotionally crippling effects were not a factor in their lives. So it was that in 1964, the Swanns took a sabbatical from their missionary duties, returning to Charlotte with a passionate new understanding of the way the world could be. The vision coexisted uneasily with the searing image of Dorothy Counts at Harding High School, but the Swanns believed—indeed with a deep certainty nurtured by a decade in India, they *knew*—that the hatred in the faces of the youthful white mob did not have to be there.

They became active in the movement to transform Southern life—the voter registration drives and other protests of the era—but their decision to file suit against the Charlotte public schools was something even more urgent and personal than a generalized pursuit of the dream of social justice. It came down to this: Their oldest child, James, was six years old when the Swanns returned to Charlotte, ready for the first grade, and they were pleased that the nearest school, which they assumed he would attend, was racially integrated. After the first day of classes, however, they were informed without apology that they lived in the gerrymandered district of an all-black school. They tried to explain to the school officials downtown, to make them understand their vision, born in India, of the necessity and rectitude of racial integration. But the school officials had never been to India, and if they were not openly hostile to the notion of integration, they did not share the Swanns' passionate belief in the urgency of it. In desperation, Darius and Vera Swann filed a lawsuit.

The results of it were little noticed for awhile. The suit made its way slowly through the federal court system, producing one ruling in 1965 that had limited effect on the Charlotte-Mecklenburg schools. But then in 1968, the case was reopened before a new federal judge, a soft-spoken Presbyterian named James B. McMillan, who, in 1969, ordered Charlotte-Mecklenburg officials to eliminate all racially identifiable schools, using busing, if necessary, since nothing else seemed to work.

The ruling became a national precedent when the Supreme Court upheld it in 1971, and suddenly, with the means now at hand to achieve complete integration, the whole nation was confronted with its conscience. In general, the nation flinched. In many large cities outside the South, busing was never tested in a way that really mattered. For reasons considered later in this volume, affluent whites and those of the upper middle class were too often able to escape the experiment, and largely as a result, busing is now widely viewed as a failure—not only by the traditional resisters to the cause of integration, but by many black leaders and white liberals as well.

In Charlotte, however, the story has been different. In the beginning, to be sure, the old instincts for ugliness rose quickly to the surface. Mobs of white protesters regularly assembled at the school system's headquarters. They hanged Judge McMillan in effigy and threatened his life, and they burned down the offices of attorney Julius Chambers, the brilliant young black man who had represented the Swanns. Gradually, however, the climate began to change, as a new generation of leaders stepped forward. For the most part, they were grass-roots people with no official standing, nothing to give them power or influence except a growing sense of hope—an ability to peer into the future and imagine how the schools might function if the people of Charlotte really embraced integration, rather than continuing the futile fight against it. Out of that perception, a new consensus formed, and in the years since then Charlotte has fundamentally changed. By almost any measure, the schools are working well. Test scores have risen; white flight is minor; parental involvement is high. But the changes have not been limited to the public school system. Sam Smith, a Republican businessman and neighborhood activist, is one of many local leaders who contend that the lawsuit filed by Darius Swann compelled the city to come to terms with the issue of race.

In the altered political climate that resulted, Smith forged a coalition with other neighborhood leaders, black and white, and in 1977, they pushed through a referendum to change Charlotte's form of government. From a city council whose representatives were all elected at large (and who were almost exclusively white businessmen), Charlotte turned to a system of district representation. In the years that followed, a vigorous, two-party democracy developed, with power widely shared. The city council in 1986 included six women, five men, six Democrats, five Republicans. The mayor pro tem was Jewish, and the mayor, Harvey Gantt, was black—a civil rights pioneer who, before losing office in 1987, had defeated strong Republican candidates in 1983 and 1985, immediately before and after Ronald Reagan's landslide.

Darius Swann was not around for most of those changes. He had left Charlotte in 1967 to continue his career as a missionary. But he returned for a visit in 1986, a tall and white-haired man of sixty-two, gentle in his manner, but emphatic in his convictions, now tempered with the disillusionment acquired in other places. "People ask me," he said, "whether I still believe in integration. I answer very guardedly. I believe in the integration that I believed in originally: We come together from different backgrounds, all sharing the gifts that we can offer to a richer society. *I don't believe* in taking a few black children and plopping them down in a white school where none of what they bring with them is accepted. I look at the country as a whole, and I wonder how much longer it will take for everybody to be free and equal. But I look at Charlotte, and I feel pleased. There have been some fundamental changes in the city, and that is what we hoped for."

But the question, he implies, is whether, even in Charlotte, the changes can be preserved—whether new generations and more recent arrivals will understand what they cost, or why busing and integration are still worth the price.

I

The Beginnings

1

September 1957

It was always a city of two minds about itself. As Dorothy Counts discovered, on September 4, 1957, while the mob of white people closed in around her, with their threats and petty violence and cries of "nigger," Charlotte was a deeply Southern city. It was caught up in all the prejudice and racial fear that defined life in the region, and those emotions, being powerful and basic, were easily stirred. But even at the time, there were glimmers of something different. Brock Barkley, a florid, barrel-chested, chain-smoking lawyer—a man of great intensity and conviction who had once chaired the school board and was now its attorney—had persuaded local school officials that integration was inevitable. The best course of action, he said, was to begin it voluntarily. He had relied on an argument of enlightened self-interest—"begin the process before somebody sues you"—but he found more than mere self-interest in Superintendent Elmer Garinger, who would tell his principals in the late spring and early summer of 1957: "Desegregation is not only the law, it is also right."

The history of race relations in Charlotte is the history of Garinger's point of view in a life-and-death collision with its volatile opposite. When that struggle began in 1957, black leaders had no illusions about which view was in ascendancy. Certainly, Herman Counts had none when Kelly Alexander, the head of the local NAACP, approached him the summer of 1957 and asked him to volunteer his children as desegregation pioneers. Counts, the father of four, was a family man first of all. But if he believed, as he often told his children, that they could be what they wanted to be, and go where they wanted to go, and the chains of prejudice did not have to bind them, Counts recognized that his was a view with political implications. Somebody had to be first. And if one of the pioneers had to come from his family, he probably felt the most confidence in Dorothy. The third of four children and the only daughter, she was uncommonly levelheaded for a girl of fifteen. There was a certain serenity about her that was hard to define, a feeling of confidence and optimism that may have been in part a reflection of her father's. But wherever it came from it was so deeply rooted as to be unobtrusive: she did not have to flaunt it, it was simply there.

Earlier in the summer of 1957, Dorothy had spent a week at a Presbyterian youth conference in Grinnell, Iowa, rooming with a white girl who had never encountered a black person before, not at least as an equal. The two of them had talked for many hours, exploding racial myths and developing a bond that gave Dorothy confidence about the challenge that now confronted her. "I told my father," she remembers, "that while I was in Grinnell, I met kids from all over the country, and I never felt anything in the way of hostility. I said I'm sure there were some negative feelings, but I didn't experience them while I was there, and I didn't think there would be a problem at Harding."

Herman Counts was proud of his daughter's courage, and quietly pleased with her view of human nature. He was, however, also a man who understood the risks, and he called the family together on the night of September 3, beginning the discussion with a prayer about what lay ahead. Such meetings were common in the Counts household, and they occurred most often at the dinner hour, usually between five and six, after Counts had returned home from his office on the nearby campus of Johnson C. Smith University.

Counts was a tall and imposing man, 6-feet-4 and 220 pounds, and with his dark suits, white shirts and carefully knotted ties, he carried himself with an air of great dignity. He came from a family of achievers, people who understood the realities of slavery and the system of white supremacy that became its natural heir, but who were determined nevertheless to carve out the foundations for the family's self-respect.

As Counts began to speak, gently and informally on that night in September, his words, his opening prayer, even the setting itself, all evoked a sense of the legacy he was seeking to impart. They had gathered, as it happened, around a family heirloom, a mahogany dining table handed down for generations, and though they would not have put it this way at the time, the table was a sturdy and cherished symbol of continuity and achievement. It had belonged most recently to Dorothy's great-uncle, the late headmaster of a black academy in Cheraw, South Carolina, a Presbyterian institution, later attended by Vera Swann, among others, and dedicated to the notion that blacks could make it in America. So as his wife and children quietly took their places, heads bowed and eyes closed, Herman Counts prayed briefly for unity and strength. He told the others that while Dorothy was the one who would be on the line, they must all be available to offer their support. And then he said to Dorothy: No matter what happens tomorrow, remember who you are. Remember the things that you have been taught. Hold your head up. You're the same as they are. You can do whatever you want to do.

Then the morning came, and Dorothy and her father, accompanied by a family friend, Edwin Thompkins, drove to Harding High School. They were astonished at the size of the crowd—maybe four hundred people, many of them students, clogging Cedar Street as it led to the school. Thompkins and Dorothy got out of the car, and while Herman Counts went to find a parking place, they began the short walk to the Harding gymnasium. The crowd immediately closed in around them, hatred twisting the young faces, as they spat at her and pelted her with ice, demanding that she return to the continent of her ancestors. She walked through them calmly, feeling, she remembered later, a strange mix of emotions, though oddly enough, fear was not among them. She felt enveloped, somehow, in the strength of her family and in the Sunday school certainty that God would protect her. And there was something else as well—an emotion that would have infuriated the mob, driving its members toward an even greater frenzy if they had only detected it. She felt *pity* for them, a conviction, tinged with the traces of youthful self-righteousness, but also with a genuine compassion, that they would not do these things if they had been raised better, if they had grown up in a family as loving as her own. Even that evening, as the threatening calls began (mixed with a few that were sympathetic) and carloads of white people cruised past her house, she persisted in feeling that it would be all right.

Meanwhile, the photographs of her reception that day were transmitted by the wire services throughout the world. Eventually, the events at Harding would be overshadowed by the rioting in Little Rock, Arkansas, where federal troops were required to assure the safety of eight black students at the city's Central High School. But for those who saw them, the pictures of Dorothy Counts and her youthful white tormentors were etched deeply in the mind, a testament to the ugly futility of the hour.

The next morning, she was sick. Plagued with chronic tonsillitis, Dorothy developed a sore throat and fever that would keep her home for two days, and even though her father went to school and picked up her homework assignments, word quickly spread that she was not coming back. Apparently as a result, there were no mobs to greet her when she returned to Harding on Monday. Encouraged, she went to her locker, picked up her books and moved on to class. There were a few shocked stares and murmurs of surprise, but the thing she remembers most was the silence of her teachers. They basically ignored her, even when she knew the answers to their questions and eagerly raised her hand. "That's OK," she told herself, "because they don't know what you know. You've just got to work a little harder."

She made it through the morning, and then came lunch. There were racial slurs as she waited in line, and when she got her food and sat down at a table by herself, several boys came up and threw trash on her plate. She got up quietly and went outside, walking by herself up a grassy hillside. In a little while, two white girls came up and introduced themselves. Their names were Jean King and Betty Broom, and they told her they were glad that she had come to Harding. Jean King, especially, seemed deeply affected by the meeting. Years later, she would remember the size and softness of Dorothy's eyes, the light-skinned delicacy of her youthful complexion. And she remembered also what they talked about—how they had sought to assure her that the hostility would pass. Then they settled on the grass, crinolines rustling beneath their calf-length skirts, and began pulling family pictures from their overstuffed wallets. Jean was particularly impressed with Dorothy's older brother, handsome and serious in his military uniform, and Dorothy remembers thinking that she had found a friend. When her father came to pick her up that day, and asked her how it had gone, she told him she was encouraged. "I had a good experience," she said, and she told him about the noon hour spent on the hillside.

Then came the third day—and things were suddenly worse. There was more pushing and shoving in the halls, more name calling, teachers still treating her as if she wasn't there. At lunchtime, she looked for Jean and Betty, who seemed to ignore her. Puzzled, she walked outside, where the two girls stopped her and told her that they would have to back away. The pressure and the ostracism were simply too great. Jean King thought for a moment that Dorothy might cry. But she didn't. She told them instead that she understood what they were saying, and that she would always remember their generosity and kindness.

The next day, the fourth, was the worst and the last. Devoid of allies, Dorothy discovered that morning that her locker had been ransacked. There were more racial slurs as she walked through the halls, more pointed silences from her teachers in class. Later at her locker, a small tin missile struck her in the head, and a blackboard eraser, thrown by a student, hit her in the back. Her brother, waiting in the car to pick her up for lunch, was startled by the shattering of the rear windshield—crushed by a mock orange, a hard piece of fruit, thrown from nearby.

Herman Counts hurried home as soon as he heard the news. He called several friends, including his minister Dr. J. W. Smith, Kelly Alexander of the NAACP, and Dr. Reginald Hawkins, a fiery young dentist who was beginning to emerge as Charlotte's leading black militant. They talked to Dorothy and discussed it among themselves, and with the concurrence of the others, Herman Counts decided that enough was enough. He turned to Dorothy, a full participant in the discussions, and told her simply: "Dot, I really don't think it's worth it."

The next day, Thursday, September 12, Counts called a press conference and issued a written statement, explaining his decision in the simplest terms:

> It is with compassion for our native land and love for our daughter Dorothy that we withdraw her as a student at Harding High School. As long as we felt she could be protected from bodily injury and insults within the school's walls and upon the school premises, we were willing to grant her desire to study at

Harding. . . . Contrary to this optimistic view, her experiences at school on Wednesday disillusioned our faith and left us no alternative.

In enrolling Dorothy in Harding High School, we sought for her the highest in educational experience that this tax supported school had to offer a young American. Yet, when a continuous stream of abuses undermines this objective our purposes are nullified and the effects are damaging to ethical and religious training.

Needless to say we regret the necessity which makes the withdrawal expedient. This step, taken for security and happiness, records in our history a page which no true American can read with pride.

Dorothy has received communications from hundreds of Americans and from at least a dozen foreign countries since her first day at Harding High School. This indicates that this historic event will be read simultaneously in England, Holland, Korea, and Charlotte—reflecting credit or discredit according to the individual's understanding of and attitude toward American democracy.

In view of this fact, we wish to express our most sincere gratitude to the many friends of democracy and Christianity in America and abroad, for their understanding and appreciation of our daughter's modest efforts to enjoy full citizenship in the country which we all love.

The true heart of America and the faith in human rights expressed by telegrams, telephone calls, local police power, and letters from friends in America and foreign countries comfort us and strengthen our belief that our cause is just and ultimately must win.

Herman Counts's last sentence has proven to be prophetic. Harding High School, now fully integrated, has been moved to a new location farther from the inner city. The old building, the site of Dorothy's ordeal, now houses Irwin Avenue Elementary, a public school nestled between the integrated neighborhoods of Third Ward and Fourth Ward, home to such black leaders as Charlotte's former mayor Harvey Gantt and former state senator Mel Watt. So strong is Irwin Avenue's academic reputation that white and black parents from all over Charlotte clamor to have their children admitted. One of Irwin's students is Jonathan Counts, Dorothy's nephew, whose mother, Stephanie Counts, is principal of another Charlotte school. Dorothy herself, now the operator of a day-care center, lives on the outskirts of the city, a welcome, respected resident of a prosperous neighborhood that is nearly all white.

But such developments were still far in the future in 1957, and Herman Counts, having taken steps to assure his daughter's physical safety, now turned his attention to the emotional scars. He was concerned first of all with her fear that she had failed. "You didn't," he told her flatly. And he was determined also that she avoid a generalized bitterness toward everybody white. While she showed no symptoms of feeling that way, Counts was concerned about the future—concerned that an anger, carefully overlaid and controlled by a maturity far beyond the capacity of most adolescents, might eventually rear its head, tearing at his daughter and causing her the kind of internal pain from which escape is difficult, if it is possible at all.

So he arranged for Dorothy to spend the school year with friends in Philadelphia, Pennsylvania, attending mostly white Yeadon High School on the outskirts of the city. Before her arrival, the principal at Yeadon called a meeting of the student body, explaining what Dorothy had been through at Harding, but telling the students, in effect, that she was no different from anybody else and they should treat her just the same.

The year went well, and the friendships she formed over the next eight or nine months were a sturdy consolation against the hard times at Harding. But there had been other consolations as well—other heartening expressions and demonstrations of good will—and several of them had come from much closer to home. Evangelist Billy Graham, for example, a Charlotte native who had already made public his opposition to segregation (in 1952, he had personally pulled down the ropes separating the white and black audiences at a Graham crusade in Chattanooga, Tennessee), sat down after reading the newspaper accounts of Dorothy's first day at Harding and wrote her a postcard. Dated September 6, 1957, and written in pencil, the message was stiff and awkwardly sympathetic, a curious mixture of Christian compassion and Cold War patriotism: "Dear Miss Counts," Graham wrote. "Democracy demands that *you* hold fast and carry on. The world of tomorrow is looking for *leaders* and you have been chosen. Those cowardly whites against you will never prosper because they are un-American and unfit to lead. Be of good faith. God is not dead. He will see you through. This is your one great chance to prove to Russia that democracy still prevails. Billy Graham, D.D."

Far more touching, and more gently Christian, was a much longer letter from Mary Bowers MacKorell, a Presbyterian Sunday school teacher who also taught Bible classes at Harding. Apologizing for an illness that had kept her away from school during much of Dorothy's ordeal, Miss MacKorell wrote on September 13:

> Dear Dorothy, I thought things were going to be all right for you at Harding. I am writing this note just to tell you how deeply I regret to hear of the events there this week which have caused you and your family to think it wise that you withdraw from our school. I can well understand your decision in this matter and do not blame you for it. You have made a very courageous and dignified effort to serve your people in this just and righteous cause. Your efforts will not be in vain for as your father so well expressed it in his excellent statement for your family, the cause is just and it will win. Perhaps the victory will be slow in coming, for that is the way God's kingdom moves forward on this earth. When I return to my Bible classes at Harding it will be with an ache in my heart that we have failed you.

Three months later, just before the Christmas holidays, Dr. Frank Porter Graham, a former U.S. senator and former president of the University of North Carolina, appeared before the student body at Harding, sharing the stage with Dr. Harry P. Harding, for whom the school was named. Graham, a plain-spoken former marine who had become a symbol of humaneness in North Carolina, called Dorothy Counts "a symbol of freedom" and declared that integration was essential "if we [are] to be the leaders of the free world." Graham received an enthusiastic ovation.

However heartening that ovation may have been—whatever its foreshadowings of the eventual triumph of good will in Charlotte—the most striking, the most healing, gesture toward Dorothy Counts may have been one that occurred much later. Nearly twenty-eight years after her departure from Harding, in February of 1985, she was interviewed by a television station in Charlotte. Returning home that evening in the nearby town of Gastonia, Jean King saw the interview and the old footage from Harding, and she decided immediately to write Dorothy a letter. For years, she said, she had wanted to explain why she had withdrawn her friendship after the sharing of pictures on the Harding hillside. In the letter and the conversation that followed it, she told Dorothy the details of her own ordeal. Jean, like Dorothy, had been a new student at the school. She had come to Charlotte that summer from her hometown of Easley, South Carolina, newly married at the age of sixteen, a little nervous, perhaps, over all the changes in her life. Her childhood had been unusually free of the prejudice that afflicted most of her peers, the Southern worldview that even her young husband would begin to struggle with, and she was grateful to her parents for the example they had set. Her father, the hard-working proprietor of a tile and flooring company, simply did not believe that white people were superior to blacks, and indeed the experiences of Jean's childhood suggested otherwise. Several of the neighborhood children were Negroes, and they were, as Jean remembered them, "high-caliber people," one of them growing up to be a doctor, another a psychologist. So when Jean King spoke warmly to Dorothy Counts on her first day at Harding, or when she admired Dorothy's family pictures several days later, she did not intend either act as a political gesture. She simply felt compassion for a girl who was the brunt of such rudeness, and in a way that was hard to define at the time, she identified with Dorothy: Dorothy was black, Jean was married, and that made them both different.

But such simple motives were incomprehensible to many of the white students at Harding, and bizarre rumors quickly spread: Jean King was a plant from the NAACP, a spy to monitor white resistance to integration.

Because of such perceptions, Jean's ordeal in September of 1957 was nearly identical to that of Dorothy Counts. She was shoved in the hallways, eggs were thrown at her car, and rocks at her upstairs apartment. And after her picture appeared with Dorothy's, first in the Charlotte *Observer* and later in *Life* magazine, her parents were harassed in South Carolina and her husband taunted on his job at Capitol Airlines. Then one day in the bathroom at Harding, other girls held the door shut and refused to let her out; and after she returned home from school, she found a menacing note attached to her door: "We know where you live." So in a frightened gesture that she has regretted ever since, Jean King told Dorothy that they could not be friends. ("I was sixteen," she says. "I wasn't mature enough to cope with it.") But they *are* friends—a happy and symbolic ending to a story that began in a very different way. As the years would reveal, it was both the blessing and the curse of Southern life that the noblest instincts—the well-spring of humaneness that coexisted with the meanness—were buried most deeply. There were places where, in time, those instincts would rise to the surface, but never easily, and never without a defeat of the ugliness in the way.

Dorothy Counts was one of four that year. Delores Maxine Huntley, a seventh grader, broke the color barrier without serious incident at Alexander Graham Junior High School. Girvaud Roberts, another seventh grader, was the object of stares and a few catcalls at Piedmont Junior High, but in general, her reception was peaceful. There were tense moments, however, for her brother, Gus Roberts, a slightly built sophomore, who was assigned to Central High School. Indeed, had it not been for the forceful intervention of Central's principal, Ed Sanders, Roberts's experiences might well have paralleled those of Dorothy Counts.

While it would not be the last time that Sanders would play such a role, he seemed, even years later, an unlikely hero in the cause of integration. Born in Greenville, South Carolina, in 1921, he was, he says, "a typical Southern boy raised in a community where the races didn't mix," a city where blacks were second-class citizens and few if any whites saw problems with the arrangement. Sanders's entry into the field of education was largely a matter of chance. He was a freshman at Furman University in 1939 when his father, a railroad depot agent, died and left the family without a lot of money, having put seven children through college in the middle of the Depression. To help see the others through, Sanders dropped out of school and went to work in a cotton mill. There, he says, he met a great many intelligent people who were totally uneducated, loom fixers, weavers, etc., and he began to ask himself what these people could accomplish if they had a little learning. "So I took a great deal of delight," Sanders remembers, "in going down early to the mill and trying to teach people something about mathematics—primarily math, and what little I could impart about the written language."

He entered the Air Force during World War II, and immediately after his discharge—the next day, in fact—he reentered Furman and began work on a teaching certificate. He came to Charlotte in 1951 to teach math and history at Central High School. He was promoted to principal in 1954, the same year that the U.S. Supreme Court handed down its historic ruling on school desegregation, and it occurred to him then that whether he liked it or not, the time would surely come when the implications of that ruling would be felt at his school. But Sanders was in no hurry. He was not a crusader by nature, and even though he no longer believed in stringent segregation (his brush with integration in the Air Force had cured him of that) it would have suited him fine to avoid the role of pioneer.

In the summer of 1957, however, Superintendent Elmer Garinger called him in for a conference. Sanders regarded Dr. Garinger with a respect that bordered on reverence. The superintendent was a quiet and unassuming man, a fatherly presence, in Sanders's estimation, and on that particular day in July, Garinger clearly had something serious on his mind. He said the decision had been made, and there was a strong possibility that one or more black children, handpicked for their ability and character, would be assigned to Central High School. Garinger was clear about his own views on the subject. Desegregation was the law, he said. It was also the right thing to do, and despite any confusion or discomfort that it might soon cause, Charlotte, North Carolina, was going ahead with it.

As Sanders remembers the conversation, he agreed with Garinger that the time to desegregate had come, but he questioned the wisdom of beginning in senior high school. He pointed out that high school students were almost adults, that they had lived their whole lives in a segregated society, and that integrating a school would represent a full frontal assault on the customs of segregation: drinking fountains, eating facilities, everything that proponents of integration were beginning to identify as targets. Wouldn't it be better, Sanders suggested, to start with younger children?

It was quickly apparent, however, that Garinger had made up his mind. So with a feeling of resignation, Sanders dropped the argument ("maybe it was a copout anyway," he says today) and entered into the task of preparing for change. He and Garinger, along with the principals of the other schools where desegregation was planned, met first with Frank Littlejohn, the chief of police, and with two newspaper editors, Pete McKnight of the Charlotte *Observer* and Cecil Prince of the Charlotte *News*. From the editors, they secured promises of thorough, but low-key coverage, and from Chief Littlejohn they received heartening assurances of total cooperation.

Littlejohn, never known as a great friend of blacks, was a tall and craggy-faced law-and-order cop, always a little bit disheveled, it seemed, but a man of great tenacity. The chief was particularly concerned about a White Citizen's Council organizer named John Kasper, who had begun to hold mass meetings in Charlotte and who had emerged as an advocate of all-out resistance. (One of Kasper's lieutenants, Mrs. John Z. Warlick, would appear at Harding High School on September 4, exhorting white students as Dorothy Counts arrived, "Spit on her, girls! Spit on her!") Regarding Kasper himself, Littlejohn told the principals, according to one account, "If that guy even walks on the lawn, we'll arrest him." Publicly, the chief's demeanor was calm and very firm. "We expect no disorder when the schools are opened tomorrow," he told reporters on September 3. "The vast majority of Charlotte residents are responsible, respectable, law-abiding citizens. Let no man mistake, however—we are prepared to preserve order by all necessary means should illegal incidents develop."

Certain of police and newspaper support, Sanders spent much of his time in the weeks leading up to September in meticulous preparation for the moment that lay ahead. One by one, he called in potential trouble-

makers from the Central student body—"I told them we can't be both-
ered with obstruction"—and he called a summer meeting of the football
squad. He told the players of the upcoming challenge for Central,
saying they were the leaders at the school and he expected them to set an
example for other students. Then, to assure that none of them underestimated the stakes, he told them that if they failed in their responsibility—
if they became part of the problem instead of the solution—there would
be no football season that fall.

Then, as now, Ed Sanders's physical presence was unimposing at
best. He was short and thin, with closely cropped hair, and there was a
genial informality in his thick Southern accent; and yet underneath it
there was also an edge, a toughness and determination that were seldom
underestimated. His staff, all but one of them Southerners with no
demonstrated aversion to the segregated order, held him in a regard that
was not quite awe; it was too familiar for that. But as one of his teachers,
Irving Edelman, put it, "Ed had tremendous rapport. His staff would
have done anything for him."

Sanders knew that what he was asking was not an easy thing. But he
said he expected the teachers to follow his own example, subordinating
personal reservations to a professional sense of duty. He selected
Edelman to play a leading role, to serve as Gus Roberts's homeroom
teacher, for Edelman alone had grown up in the integrated schools of
Cleveland, Ohio. Together, they planned a schedule to minimize the
physical distance between Gus's classes, and between periods, at least
one teacher, or sometimes Sanders himself, was assigned to keep
watch.

Sanders also met with Gus and his family, coordinating precisely the
times of his arrivals and departures, walking him carefully through his
day—showing him each of his classrooms, reviewing which stairs he
was to use to get from one to the other. Finally, the first day came,
September 4, and the morning brought a huge, jeering crowd in front of
the school. But Sanders knew, he says, that "people will respond to a
bell," and he rang it early, several minutes before Gus arrived with his
father at precisely nine o'clock. The crowd dispersed, and the day
passed without serious incident.

The next day, however, was a different matter. Shortly before Gus's scheduled arrival, Ed Sanders glanced out of his office and saw a chilling spectacle. A crowd of angry-looking teenagers, most of them students, had locked arms across the entrance to the school, blocking the doorway and giving no indication that the gesture was a bluff. The newspaper that morning had been filled with reports of the petty violence at Harding, and Sanders understood that such ideas are contagious. "So a decision had to be made," he remembered much later, "as to whether you go out there and try to get the boy and bring him in, or whether you get your briefcase and go home. It was that simple. It was to me. And I didn't want to get my briefcase." So with a knot of fear in his stomach, realizing that the situation now teetered on the edge of an explosion, Sanders took a breath and walked toward the students. He was lucky, he says. Near the middle of the chain he spotted a boy who had recently been in a scrape with the law and for whom Sanders had testified in court. He approached the young man and said in a voice that was matter-of-fact on the surface, but unmistakable in the threat that it implied, "Let me through here." The chain parted, and Sanders passed through to meet Gus Roberts at the curb. As the two of them turned toward the building, however, the crowd was beginning to regain its nerve, reassembling in front of the door. Somebody knocked Gus's cap off his head—an act of defiance, Sanders knew, that could lead to escalation. "Pick it up," he said, and again his tone suggested the request was not idle. The offending student did not move, and for an agonizing second the cap lay on the ground. But then another student, not party to the resistance, picked up the cap and returned it to Gus. The tension subsided, and Roberts and Ed Sanders moved on to class.

Irving Edelman was a witness to the scene, and he understood the delicacy and the subtlety of it. He marveled at Sanders's leadership, respecting not so much his charisma or his coolness as his overarching sense of duty. He knew also that there were no role models for Sanders to follow, for in 1957 there were few if any public school principals who had successfully confronted a situation as racially charged as the one at Central High School.

But if Sanders was one of the heroes of the story, and if he continued to perform that way, another undeniably was Gus Roberts himself. Shy and introverted, but quietly courageous, he evoked, almost from the beginning, a sense of protectiveness among many of Central's students. There were occasional incidents of pushing and physical harassment (one in which Gus's head was cut by a swinging library door; the student who did the shoving was suspended), but in general many of Gus's peers, who had never confronted a black person as an equal, found themselves drawn to his unassuming manner.

In the years that followed, Irving Edelman would argue frequently that Central's story was a triumph for racial integration, arguably one of the first in the South. Ed Sanders, however, would remain more guarded in his final assessments. The year ended badly, culminating in an ugly little episode that still, nearly thirty years later, caused Sanders to wince and second-guess himself at the mere mention of it. It seems that as the day drew near for the senior prom, Gus Roberts decided that he wanted to go. As word of that decision began to spread, threatening calls began to come in, and their number was alarming. They came to Sanders, the school board, even the police, and the message was the same: if Gus Roberts goes to the prom, he will suffer bodily harm, either that night or later. Sanders took the calls seriously and called off the prom. Then a new round of calls began, and the message this time was that the decision would not do: if the prom did not go off as scheduled, *without Gus Roberts*, Gus would suffer for it.

In an interview in 1986, Sanders, now white-haired and the superintendent of schools in Darlington, South Carolina, told the story resolutely, but without enthusiasm. "This is one of the things that I don't like to remember," he said. "But I do." And he recounted how, after having taken the position for nearly a year that Gus Roberts was a student with the same rights and privileges as any other at his school, he decided that the senior prom would be a private, all-white affair, financed by contributions and held off campus. Though the decision was not indefensible and though Sanders was certain of his own motivations, he recognized the moment for what it was—a violation of his principles, forced upon him by the threat of terrorism. He remembers thinking that Charlotte had a long way to go.

2

Setting the Stage for *Swann*

Not a lot happened in the schools for the next several years. The struggle for integration shifted to other arenas, as Charlotte's black leaders, chiefly Reginald Hawkins and Kelly Alexander, began a scattergun assault on the symptoms of white supremacy. The number of blacks attending previously all-white schools increased incrementally, but Charlotte's system of education, like the community as a whole, remained essentially segregated.

One black activist who chafed most impatiently under that reality was Hawkins, formerly a college classmate of Darius Swann's and now a minister and dentist—an unlikely and demanding combination of livelihoods that typified the energy with which he pursued nearly everything. Born in Beaufort, North Carolina, Hawkins was a leader of great intelligence, representing at least the third generation of his family to make it through college. A small and round-faced man with the ferocious bearing of a bantamweight boxer, Hawkins was relentless and irrepressible in his resistance to segregation. He petitioned and demonstrated, made fiery speeches, and eventually ran for governor—all in the pursuit of black voting rights and integrated schools, desegregated hospitals, and equal access to public accommodations.

For all his brilliance and courage, however, Hawkins had one particular trait that served him badly: He seemed to be a bitter and erratic man, given to personalizing his disputes and differences of opinion, even with other blacks. As a result, he could be a divisive influence in the black community, and he provided for many whites an easy rationalization for mistrusting his motives and, if they chose, for dismissing the goals of the movement he represented.

Similar problems did not exist for Kelly Alexander, Sr., who may have been Charlotte's most important black leader. Later he would become the national board chairman of the NAACP, a reward for spending nearly a half century as one of the organization's most effective representatives. Born in Charlotte on August 18, 1915, Alexander was the youngest of five sons. He told one reporter in 1962 that his passion for civil rights began to take shape in the 1930s, after he graduated from Booker T. Washington's Tuskegee Institute and went to work for a Jewish merchant in New York City.

Alexander and his boss, Samuel Morton, barnstormed the country selling wholesale jewelry, and in the South especially, they were both the victims of racial discrimination. Unable to find hotel rooms, Alexander was often forced to spend the night in private black residences or in his car. But perhaps the most vivid indignity came one afternoon in Shreveport, Louisiana, when Samuel Morton was negotiating with a downtown jeweler, and Alexander was waiting at the car. A self-confident young man with an air of self-possession that was almost jaunty, Alexander was relaxing with one of Morton's cigars when two Shreveport policemen walked up and demanded: "Nigger, what are you doing standing out here in the street, looking like you own the town?"

Alexander was not a person who tolerated insults. He was every inch the son of Zechariah Alexander, the successful proprietor of a Charlotte funeral home, a strong and upright man with piercing eyes and a long, angular face. Zechariah was born in 1877 and came of age during the waning years of the nineteenth century, a cruel and ironic time for black people in the South, when they caught just a whiff of full citizenship, only to have it snatched away by the momentum and terrorism of resurgent white supremacy. Zack Alexander, as he was known to his friends, was determined to lay the foundation for his family to make it, to imbue his children with the notion that they were as good as anybody.

His youngest son was inclined to believe it, and buttressed by that idea, and also by the certainty that he had done nothing wrong, Kelly Alexander decided on that afternoon in Shreveport to defy the two policemen who were giving him trouble. "They told me," he remembered more than twenty years later, "to leave by the time they walked down the street and back. I didn't. When they came back, I told them who I was waiting for, and the manager of the jewelry store came and talked to them. They finally decided to let me go."

With such experiences heavy on his mind, Alexander returned to Charlotte in 1939 to help run the family business. He was also becoming an increasingly avid student of black history. From his grandmother and great-grandmother, he had heard the stories of the time when they were slaves, and from his father and other sources, he had learned of the Klan's bitter legacy near the turn of the century. He regarded the capricious hostility of the Shreveport police—and the other acts of intimidation to which blacks were subjected—as merely an extension of that history. He vowed to do what he could to write a different chapter.

In 1940, Alexander founded a local branch of the NAACP and threw himself into the task of building a black movement, recruiting members for his new organization, and, over the years, bringing to Charlotte nearly every black leader of the era: Thurgood Marshall, Roy Wilkins, Clarence Mitchell, Adam Clayton Powell, Ralph Abernathy, and later, Martin Luther King. By the mid-1950s, Alexander had also established himself as an implacable public opponent of segregation, and his name began to appear regularly in the Charlotte newspapers. In 1956, for example, a young Charlotte *News* reporter named Charles Kuralt wrote dispassionately of Alexander's opposition to a segregated Ice Capades performance at the Charlotte Coliseum. And in March of 1957, Alexander made headlines again with one of the most important undertakings of his civil rights career. On March 29, he led a delegation of twenty-six blacks, including his friend Reginald Hawkins, to a meeting with officials of Charlotte's public schools. The subject of the meeting was desegregation, and while the blacks received evasive answers at the time, the officials were moving toward a momentous decision. Recognizing the inevitability of Alexander's demand, they agreed to work over the next several months with their counterparts in Winston-Salem and Greensboro to desegregate the schools in all three cities. The result was the entry of Dorothy Counts into Harding High School and Gus Roberts into Central.

In that undertaking and many others, Alexander and Hawkins were the recognized leaders of the Charlotte black community, and for much of their careers, the two men were close friends. Hawkins was a frequent dinner guest in the Alexander home, particularly when black dignitaries came to town, for both men were nationally respected for their courage and commitment. After a time, however, a rivalry began to simmer, and it became public in 1962 when they disagreed pointedly about the most effective voting strategy for blacks. Even then, however, the two continued to share a common agenda, attacking white supremacy at every seam they could find, with school desegregation simply one of many issues.

By the early 1960s they had been joined in their efforts by two other key figures. The first was Fred Alexander, Kelly's older brother, a man of great political skill and diplomatic smoothness, who soon emerged as Charlotte's most visible black leader. In 1965, he became the first black city councilman since Reconstruction. He was mayor pro tem in 1973 and was elected to the state senate in 1975. Meanwhile, the other critical addition to the roster of black leaders was a young attorney named Julius Chambers. A native of Mt. Gilead, North Carolina, a farming community on the fringes of the Piedmont, Chambers came to Charlotte in 1964. Quiet, almost taciturn, he set up offices in a rented cold-water flat at 405½ East Trade Street, a string of three barren rooms above a savings and loan office. Chambers was a man of uncommon energy, meticulous in his preparation, and cool in the courtroom. He provided for blacks in Charlotte the legal brilliance that their movement had lacked, and together with Reginald Hawkins and the two Alexanders, he rounded out the first tier of a formidable leadership structure that was tenacious, impatient, but fundamentally reasonable.

It was also not without its white allies. Easily the most colorful and nationally prominent of those was a Jewish author named Harry Golden, who, from 1942 until a serious illness in 1968, edited a bimonthly paper called the *Carolina Israelite*. The son of European immigrants (his mother was Romanian, his father, Austrian), Golden grew up in New York City. He rebelled, while he was young, against the orthodox Jewishness practiced by his parents, particularly his mother. But the ravages of Hitler in the thirties and forties left him with an acute awareness of his own ethnic roots. He wrote about them with great eloquence and occasional sentimentality in his little newspaper, declaring, for example, in the January issue of 1957: "I haven't the slightest worry about the future of Israel. The Egyptians will not beat her, nor will the entire Arab world, nor even the whole Soviet Union. It is impossible to beat a people who go into the desert, with the Bible in their hands, and the leader says, 'There was a spring here in the days of King Solomon—start digging.' "

Many of Golden's readers—there were thirty thousand of them scattered around the world, each of them paying two dollars a year—were startled at such a voice emanating from the South, and Golden began to move easily and with relish through the realms of the famous. He became a frequent guest on the "Jack Paar Show" and a visitor to the White House during several administrations. Never afflicted with an excessive sense of modesty, he plastered his walls with pictures and memorabilia, mostly photographs of himself with David Ben-Gurion, Eleanor Roosevelt, Carl Sandburg, and all three Kennedys.

Mixed in with the displays of ego and the flashes of seriousness, there was also a comic quality about Golden's style. It was there even in his appearance: the suspenders, the oversized cigars, the twinkle in his eye behind the dark-rimmed glasses. Perhaps that is why he could get away with something far more threatening, far more subversive in the South of his day, than ringing proclamations about his own Jewish heritage. Between the 1940s and the late 1960s, Golden emerged as one of the nation's leading opponents of white supremacy, and he did it with satire. He mocked the hallowed institution of racial segregation. His most famous essay was written in the summer of 1956. It was a proposal for what he called the Golden Vertical Negro Plan, a modest suggestion, Golden said, for the North Carolina legislature and others in the South then debating what to do about school desegregation. Golden's reasoning went like this:

> The white and Negro races stand at the same grocery and super market counters, deposit money at the same bank-teller's window, pay taxes, light and phone bills to the same clerks, walk through the same dime and department stores, and stand at the same drug-store counter. It is only when the Negro sits down that the folks become panicky. Now since the South is not even think-

ing of restoring vertical racial segregation, I think my plan would fulfill our three requirements of the moment: (a) Comply with the Supreme Court decisions, (b) save our public schools and (c) maintain sitting-down segregation. Now here is the Golden Vertical Negro Plan. Instead of all these complicated and costly proposals, all the Special Session needs to do is pass one small amendment to provide only desks in all our public schools, no seats. The desks should be the stand-up type, like the old-fashioned bookkeeping desk. Since no one in the South pays the slightest attention to a Vertical Negro, this would solve our problem completely. . . . In every direction the Golden Vertical Negro Plan will save millions of dollars, and forever eliminate any danger to our public education system, upon which rests the destiny, the hopes, and the happiness of this society.

It is difficult to say what impact Golden had on Charlotte. He was not especially popular or honored in the city. But he did push his case with cleverness and tenacity, making the leap with ease from his concern over the oppression of Jews in Europe to the oppression of blacks in America. And his very outrageousness may have added legitimacy to more moderate voices. As his longtime friend Anita Brown put it, "Harry sort of softened people up."

Another Charlottean who believed Golden helped legitimize the discussion of integration—and whose own views seemed less radical by comparison—was Pete McKnight, a young North Carolina native who edited the Charlotte _News_ from 1948 to 1954 and the Charlotte _Observer_ from 1955 to 1976. McKnight, like Golden, could feel the changes in the air, and he thought early on that the most crucial arena might well be the schools.

McKnight was born in Shelby, fifty miles from Charlotte, and he took early offense at the segregated order. In a valedictory address to his high school class, he gave voice to a conviction that grew stronger with time: "Our schools," he said, "can do more than any other influence to break down the wall of prejudice. If the schools have a world-wide mission, it is to clear up the idea that some are born superior to others in human rights."

For more than twenty-five years, such views defined McKnight's tenure as an editor, and he was one of the first in the South to sense the inevitability of change. On June 7, 1950, he wrote an editorial called "Handwriting On The Wall," detailing the implications of three Supreme Court rulings handed down on June 5. The first of those was *Sweatt* v. *Painter*, the case of a black Texas mailman who wanted to become a lawyer. There were only twenty-three black lawyers in Texas at the time, and Heman Sweatt was determined to become the twenty-fourth, but on his own terms. He applied to the all-white law school at the University of Texas, and was denied admission because of his race. When Sweatt took his grievance to federal court, Texas officials decided to set up a law school especially for him, a basement branch of Prairie View University, with a faculty that consisted of two Negro lawyers. By the time Sweatt's case had reached the U.S. Supreme Court, Texas officials had added certain improvements to the Prairie View law school, specifically a library and a small student body, but Sweatt and his attorney, Thurgood Marshall, argued that the school was still inferior to its white counterpart. Marshall, who was later appointed to the U.S. Supreme Court by Lyndon Johnson, a president from Texas, was then the chief counsel for the NAACP Legal Defense Fund.

The *Sweatt* case was one piece of a cautious legal strategy that Marshall had devised. Though he longed to challenge the constitutionality of the fifty-year-old doctrine of separate but equal, a Supreme Court precedent handed down in the case of *Plessy* v. *Ferguson* in 1896, he was afraid of backing the Court into a corner and causing it to affirm once again the constitutionality of segregation. Indirection thus became Marshall's strategy. He was determined to demonstrate that separate but equal was a fiction. Separation was real, but equality was not, and the easiest, least expensive way to rectify the problem was to end segregation.

The *Sweatt* case was a good one in that context; the law school facilities made available to Heman Sweatt were clearly not comparable to those afforded whites. A riskier undertaking was the case of George McLaurin, a black graduate student recently admitted to the University of Oklahoma, but carefully segregated within the university. McLaurin was required to sit, eat, even study at the library in areas roped off or designated for blacks. It was clearly insulting, but was it illegal? McLaurin, unlike Sweatt, was provided with the same professors, books, and other academic resources that were offered to whites. Similar questions were raised by the case of Elmer Henderson, a black employee of the federal government, who, on a train trip to the South, was required to eat in a "Colored Only" section of the dining car. The menu was the same, and so were the prices; the indignity was simply that he was made to sit apart.

In June of 1950, when the Supreme Court ruled unanimously for the blacks in all three cases, Pete McKnight responded with a long, thoughtful, and well-informed editorial:

> Three important Supreme Court decisions chipped away at the structure of racial segregation without actually demolishing it. . . . We are devoting so much space to this topic today because we think it is of paramount importance. North Carolina already faces four test suits. One demands the admittance of Negroes to the University of North Carolina law school. Three demand equal facilities in the public schools, or else the abolition of segregation. . . .
>
> We have said it before. We say it again today. Segregation, as an abstract moral principle, can not be defended by any intellectually or spiritually honest person. Yet we are dealing with more than an abstract moral principle. We are dealing with the realities of a system which dates back many generations. That system can not be overturned by Congressional act or judicial interpretation without causing a degree of chaos that probably would be more detrimental to the national welfare and to that of the nation's citizens than a continuance of segregation would be. It can, however, be worn down, bit by bit.
>
> Hence, we are torn between gratification that the Supreme Court is gradually giving us a better standard for measuring real American democracy and apprehension that the Court or Congress might go too fast.
>
> That having been said, we remind Tar Heels that the handwriting is on the wall. . . . The Supreme Court may leave the "sepa-

rate but equal" facilities on the books. But our state will have to get busy and make the facilities truly equal if it hopes to maintain racial segregation.

Within a year or two, McKnight was convinced that segregation was beyond all redemption, no matter how sweeping the reforms. He was familiar with a case in South Carolina, in which a group of black parents in rural Clarendon County had petitioned school officials to provide a bus for their children. After all, the blacks reasoned, bus transportation was available to white students. But such was the prejudice in Clarendon County that the request by the parents was treated as extreme. "We ain't got no money to provide a bus for your nigger children," one official said. Stung by the rebuff and the salt in the wounds, the parents called Thurgood Marshall and filed a lawsuit, eventually escalating their demands into a frontal assault on racial segregation. In 1954, the Clarendon case was combined with four others, and the Supreme Court ruled in the black parents' favor: segregated schools were inherently unequal, and *Plessy* v. *Ferguson* was no longer the law.

For black Americans generally, the ruling was a victory, perhaps the greatest in nearly a hundred years. But in Clarendon County, they paid a price for it. Whites withdrew from the public schools entirely, and blacks whose names were attached to the suit often faced economic or physical reprisals. Their leader, a minister named J. A. DeLaine, was driven from the county by terrorist gunfire, and nearly thirty years later, his widow Mattie, who had since moved to Charlotte, remembered the fear on the night that he left: "They were driving by in cars," she said, speaking softly, with just a hint of old emotions still in her voice,

> a gang of people shooting toward the house. You could see the dust flying from where the bullets hit. My husband said, "Go to bed. They're not going to do anything. They just want to scare somebody." But they came back, shooting again, and he decided this time to shoot back. Then he knew he had to leave. He got in his car and drove away. I didn't know where he had gone. He was in New York when I heard from him again.
>
> I got on a train to meet him there. I couldn't sleep that night. As we rolled through Virginia—I guess it was Virginia—every-

body else was asleep except me. I was watching the woods outside. It was fall, and even at night you could see the color. And that's when it came to me. It was almost like a voice saying, "He who rules that beautiful scenery out there will rule your life." I kept listening, and the tears were streaming down my face, and the voice was saying: "So don't have hate for anybody." And I don't. I don't have hate in my heart for a single person.

My husband, though, he was a little bit different. He didn't hate. He was too nice a person. But he wouldn't let anybody take advantage. When he saw the unfairness, there was just something in him that made him speak out. I don't know. That's just the way he was.

Pete McKnight was moved by the story, and he respected the courage of people like J. A. DeLaine. But McKnight was a white man, civic-minded and prominent, and as such he was moved by something else as well. Though many of his contemporaries regarded him as a liberal, his basic motivation was conservative to the bone. He wanted to preserve the domestic tranquility of his city—a goal, he knew, that made it imperative to give ground gradually.

By the early 1960s, McKnight was not alone in holding that view. Charlotte's mayor Stan Brookshire had also begun to see the writing on the wall, for indeed by then it was difficult to miss. Demonstrations and violent reprisals had stained the image of Birmingham, Alabama. In May of 1963, Birmingham blacks were entering the twelfth month of a boycott of downtown businesses, demanding an end to segregated public accommodations. The city's mood was ugly. There had been several bombings in the black community, the school board had suspended 1,081 black students who had participated in peaceful protests, and Mayor Arthur Hanes had joined police commissioner Bull Connor in calling for a white boycott in defense of segregation, if the business community caved in to blacks.

Meanwhile, the headlines closer to home were nearly as dramatic. In Raleigh there were eight days of demonstrations in early May, and in Durham, 415 blacks were arrested on May 19. But the greatest national scrutiny was focused on Greensboro, where the sit-in movement began in 1960, and where it was still in full force in 1963. On May 16, more than 500 blacks demonstrated at the segregated S&W Cafeteria, prompting 150 arrests, and by May 23, the number of demonstrators had swelled to 4,000. White leaders in Charlotte were keeping careful track of these events, feeling more edgy as time went by—especially after May 20, when Reginald Hawkins led what the Charlotte *Observer* called "a spirited, but orderly band of singing, hand-clapping Negro students" on a march through downtown.

"I called Stan Brookshire," Pete McKnight remembered years later, "and told him, 'if you want to keep Charlotte out of the headlines of the *New York Times*,'" the leadership must take concerted action. Brookshire agreed, and immediately asked Chamber of Commerce president Ed Burnside to call a meeting. On May 23, after a preliminary discussion within the Chamber's executive committee, two dozen Chamber directors met for lunch at the prestigious (and segregated) Charlotte City Club, where they were presented with a resolution drafted mostly by McKnight. The resolution, calling for voluntary desegregation of public accommodations, passed unanimously and without debate. But Burnside wanted to make certain the consensus was solid. "This means," he said, "that every man in this room thinks we have taken the right step." Again, there was no dissent.

Immediately after the meeting, Chamber leaders began a series of conversations with key representatives among Charlotte's hotel and restaurant owners, seeking support for the Chamber resolution. They got it. One of the owners, Slug Claiborne, suggested what amounted to an odd modification of black sit-in tactics—that white business leaders ask groups of black leaders to lunch, thus setting a tone for the rest of the community. McKnight, meanwhile, wrote an editorial, detailing his view of the city's responsibilities: "It's time to give more than is asked, to reduce our racial enmities by making them into friendships." The combined efforts were successful, and by August, fully a year before the 1964 Civil Rights Act made it a matter of law, Charlotte had largely desegregated its public accommodations.

Cynics were inclined to dismiss all of that as a preoccupation with image that was economic at its core—Chamber of Commerce cosmetology on the city's best face. There was, of course, some truth to that view. But Pete McKnight believed that whatever its origin, there was also a larger spirit in Charlotte. It was not a *liberal* city with a passion to integrate; on the contrary, there was a simple civic pride that was fundamentally old-fashioned, fundamentally conservative in its concern for social order. But there were leaders who understood that order was threatened by the absence of progress, and they were determined to see that Charlotte did not come apart.

"I don't know where it came from," McKnight would remember much later, shortly before his death in 1986. "But when I came to the city in 1939, there was a particular definition of community leadership. Money alone didn't make you prominent. You were nothing until you headed the United Way or built a Red Cross building. Maybe it was because there was no dominant industry, no dominant family, no mean or narrow oligarchy with a resistance to change. Wherever it came from, there was no prestige in Charlotte until you worked for the community."

Stan Brookshire put it a different way: "Basically," he said, "we were just too proud of Charlotte to let differences on any issue tear the town down."

As the years went by and other crises arose, particularly the agony over busing in the 1970s, the McKnight-Brookshire understanding of Charlotte would be severely tested. Later, other leaders, including many blacks, would come to share the view. But in the early 1960s, self-congratulation over the dimensions of progress remained a white man's luxury. Blacks were still compelled to live with reality.

Julius Chambers came to town in 1964, approximately a year after the desegregation of public accommodations. There were exceptions to the integrated pattern, he noted, restaurants still sullen in their service to blacks. (One that intrigued him most was a Chinese place a block or two from his office.) But if Chambers was generally pleased that he could eat where he wanted, he found Charlotte as a whole still rigidly segregated. "It was almost," he said in 1984,

like the South Africa that I saw two years ago—blacks on one side of the tracks and whites on the other; blacks realizing that they were not able to be employed as clerks, or tellers in banks, so they didn't apply. People sort of accepted that situation in 1964. Most of the time I spent in those days was going to various mass meetings, attempting to advise people about their rights and about the resources available to them. We had a real problem getting blacks to become involved in litigation because of threats, physically and to their livelihood. So we were rigidly segregated, and we had public attitudes—among blacks and whites—that that's the way society was supposed to be. It's a real educational process, getting people to look at things differently.

Chambers threw himself into that process, traveling the state end to end in a well-worn Plymouth, its odometer starting over at 100,000 miles. His new law partner, a friendly, twenty-seven-year-old white man by the name of Adam Stein, was astonished at his energy—his ability to endure the ninety-hour weeks, the staggering case load and the appearances in court, the speeches in churches and at the local gatherings of the NAACP. There were not a lot of private moments during their time in the office, but occasionally over dinner with Chambers and their wives, Stein would sift through the clues about the things that made Chambers tick. What was the source of the energy, the perfectionism, the merciless drive that he applied to himself and, with a little more leniency, to the people around him? Stein could never say for sure; Chambers was much easier to *describe* than explain, and even then he was essentially enigmatic—reserved, even-tempered, chilly in his rage at a segregated world, and above all else, it sometimes seemed, reluctant to say very much about himself. But there was one particular story that he told many times, and though it was trite in a way—almost any black man could tell a dozen like it—it seemed to have been a moment of truth, a way to personalize the indignities of the times.

On a spring afternoon in 1949, Julius Chambers, then thirteen, was sitting in the living room of his family's house, listening to his father, William Chambers, explain how the family had been cheated of two thousand dollars. Mr. Chambers had worked hard over the years to build up a business as an auto mechanic, and one of his customers was a white man who owned a trucking company. Chambers had maintained the man's rig, buying parts for it over a period of months, but earlier that day the man had refused to pay his bill, jeering as he drove away in the truck. For the rest of the day, Bill Chambers had taken his grievance from one white lawyer to another (all lawyers were white in the town of Mt. Gilead) only to be turned down. Nobody wanted to represent a colored mechanic in a dispute with a white man.

Julius Chambers was moved by his father's pain and his struggle, only partly successful, to control his emotions, and he decided then and there that he would become a lawyer. Some adolescent resolutions fall victim to the years, but Chambers's did not. He got his undergraduate degree at North Carolina College, his first law degree from the University of North Carolina (where he was the first black editor of the law review), and an advanced degree from Columbia University. He spent a year as an intern with the NAACP Legal Defense Fund, working with Jack Greenberg, the successor to Thurgood Marshall as the organization's chief counsel, and from there he came to Charlotte, arriving in July of 1964.

Less than two months later, he received a call from Vera Swann, whose son, a first grader, had been assigned to a segregated school, and thus began the most important case of his career. Already, in fact, Reginald Hawkins and another black leader, Ezra Moore, had visited his office to discuss the public schools. They were concerned about the closing of black schools, job security for black teachers, and the general lack of progress toward desegregation. Their concerns came at a time when Jack Greenberg and the Legal Defense Fund lawyers, with whom Chambers retained a tie, were interested in filing as many cases as they could, pushing to step up the pace of desegregation.

Specifically, they were trying to undo a precedent set in the Clarendon County case—*Briggs* v. *Elliott*, it was called—when it was sent back to the lower courts after the Supreme Court's landmark ruling of 1954. Charged with overseeing the details of the county's desegregation process, Judge John J. Parker of North Carolina wrote that the 1954 decision did not require integration; it simply forbade segregation—the active, deliberate separation of children by race. Once the segregation requirement was removed, in Judge Parker's view, the Constitutional issue was settled. Chambers and the other Legal Defense Fund lawyers were seeking new rulings overturning Judge Parker—rulings that would require school districts to take affirmative steps to root out the old patterns of racial separation.

The purposes of Vera Swann and her husband Darius were less theoretical. They simply wanted their six-year-old son, James Swann, readmitted to Seversville Elementary School, which was, first of all, the closest school to their home, and more importantly, one of only six in Charlotte where the level of integration was more than token.

When the Swanns had returned to North Carolina, after their eleven years as missionaries to India, they had been surprised and disappointed at the glacial pace of integration. On the opening day of school in 1964, seven years after Dorothy Counts and Gus Roberts had broken the barrier, there were still eighty-eight one-race schools in Charlotte—fifty-seven all white and thirty-one all black. Only twenty-one schools were integrated, and of those only six had more than a dozen black students. The depressing numbers continued: of Charlotte's more than 20,000 black students, only 822 were in school with whites, and even that total was inflated by the fact that eleven white students, the last holdouts in a changing neighborhood, had joined 374 blacks at Bethune Elementary.

After years in a multiracial community of missionaries in India, where American racism seemed a distant and nearly inexplicable aberration, the Swanns were convinced of the redeeming power of integration. As Christians they were concerned for the family of man, and as parents they were concerned for their son—and for all of those reasons, they had decided even before they came back to Charlotte that they would not participate in a system of segregation.

For a brief time it appeared they would not have to. They called the school board shortly after their return and asked where James should report on the first day of class. "To the nearest school," they were told, and the Swanns were delighted. The closest school to their house was Seversville Elementary, which had 297 white students and 26 blacks. James would have been the 27th. But when he came home on the first afternoon, August 31, the boy carried with him a polite and apologetic note from the principal. He was in the wrong school, the note explained simply. He lived in the district for Biddleville Elementary, which was, unfortunately, an all-black school.

On September 2, Darius Swann wrote a letter to the board of education, neatly typed, single spaced, and urgent in its pleading: "We believe that an integrated school will best prepare young people for responsibility in an integrated society. Having lived practically all of his life in India, James has never known the meaning of racial segregation. We have been happy to watch him grow and develop with an unaffected openness to people of all races and backgrounds, and we feel it our duty as parents to insure that this healthy development continue. James attended Seversville briefly on August 31 and he liked the school and its atmosphere. We did also and feel that this is where we would like him to be." Swann also reminded the board of what would soon become an uncontested legal fact: students in the Charlotte-Mecklenburg schools were frequently and routinely allowed to transfer out of integrated schools, but not in the opposite direction. "We hold that the law should be equally binding . . ." Swann wrote. "Otherwise the law is discriminatory."

After her husband's letter, Vera Swann asked for a meeting with Superintendent Craig Phillips, who had replaced Elmer Garinger in 1962. Accompanied by Reginald Hawkins, a family friend, she paid a visit to Phillips's office on September 3. She couldn't help but be a little bit impressed with the new superintendent. At least most people were. He was a handsome, lean-faced man with a dignified touch of gray at his temples, and there was something commanding about him—a thoughtful self-confidence, softened by his smile. It was also true that he was not a segregationist. Indeed, he had stepped up the pace of integration quite markedly in the short time since his arrival in Charlotte (which was not hard to do, as the number of black children in school with whites had actually *dropped* in the first four years—from four in the fall of 1957 to two in the spring of 1961). The fall of 1964 brought what Phillips regarded as a significant improvement, and though the numbers were still unimpressive to blacks, the superintendent was pleased with the progress, for he measured it against the realities of the past. On August 21, speaking with the forceful informality that had become his trademark, he had told a group of principals: "This will be the most significant year so far in the integration of our youngsters. I want you to be aware, to work with parents' groups and teachers as you have done in the past. I emphasize the need to carry this responsibility and carry it well."

In the matter of Vera Swann and her son, however, Phillips and William Anderson, the serious and bureaucratic assistant superintendent who was with him for the meeting, decided to pass the buck. They suggested to Mrs. Swann that she take her case to the school board, and on September 9, the board rejected her request. Frustrated, she asked Reginald Hawkins to find her a lawyer, and she remembers very clearly her first meeting with Julius Chambers: he impressed her as distant, reserved, severely professional, asking difficult questions with demanding dispassion. The Swanns developed a deep respect for him, however, as the weeks of preparation turned into months, and nine other families joined them in the case. Chambers was meticulous, energetic, and bold, and when the case was filed, on January 19, 1965, the Swanns were optimistic.

In fact, for them the results were immediate. In response to the suit, the school board began work on a new desegregation plan, using freedom of choice as one of its components and ushering in the only period in the modern history of Charlotte's schools where busing for racial purposes was not a fact of daily life; before 1965, it was busing to achieve segregation, later it was busing to achieve the opposite result. In the fall of 1965, the Swanns chose to send both their children, James and his younger sister Edith, to Eastover Elementary, a formerly all-white school in a prosperous neighborhood, with spreading oak trees and broad winding streets and two-story houses that looked like castles. For the next two years, until they left Charlotte in 1967, they were satisfied consumers of public education.

By then, however, the suit that they had filed was beginning to develop a life of its own, and within the next several years it would compel the people of Charlotte, black and white, to decide what kind of community they wanted theirs to be. For a time, the stakes seemed deadly.

On November 22, 1965, shortly after midnight, or maybe a little later, Kelly Alexander finally closed his book and went to bed. He had always been a man of late-night habits. His curiosity most evenings wound down rather slowly, and the stillness after midnight seemed a perfect time to read. But the stillness that night was soon disrupted. A bomb—four sticks of dynamite, the police later guessed—exploded against the front of his suburban brick house, shattering the picture window, leaving a foot-long gash near the base of the wall and sending showers of glass into the bedroom of his sons. The boys, Alfred and Kelly Jr., were both teenagers, and in the first few seconds of horror—in that fleeting time before anxiety turned to rage—Kelly Sr. had feared for their lives. The bomb exploded only a few feet from their beds, but the wall was strong and the windows in the room were unusually high, almost at the level of the ceiling. The glass exploded inward with such force that the most lethal fragments shattered against the far wall of the room, and the boys were not hurt.

Next door, meanwhile, another bomb exploded simultaneously. The target this time—again, unhurt—was Fred Alexander, Kelly's older brother, who was at home with his wife. It was 2:15. At 2:20 another bomb shattered the windows in Julius Chambers's house only a short drive away. At 2:30, the final blast sprayed glass into the bedroom of Reginald Hawkins, who heard the sound of a car speeding off into the night.

It was drizzling rain by the time the reporters and the police arrived—dozens of them, it seemed, glass crunching under their feet as they peered at the damage—and in the melancholy aftermath of the narrow escape, the four black leaders collected their thoughts. They knew that the terrorists had intended to kill them, and in that goal, were not representative of the people of Charlotte. But Hawkins, Chambers, and the two Alexanders all understood something else as well. The bombings came at a time of uncommon activity on the civil rights front: the *Swann* case, the election of Fred Alexander to the Charlotte City Council, a suit to integrate the Shrine Bowl football game (a high school all-star event played annually in the city). Many whites, many thousands, in fact, who lacked the boldness, the commitment, or the final edge of meanness to experiment with dynamite, shared, nevertheless, a nightrider's rage at the gathering black momentum. In that sense the bombings of November 22 were merely a crude exaggeration, a murderous caricature, of prevailing white opinion.

Still, there were reasons for hope. The Charlotte *Observer* offered a reward for the capture of the criminals, money was raised to help the victims rebuild, and Mayor Stan Brookshire, who had once been the target of a cross-burning himself, led the chorus of outrage from the city's white leaders. Seventy-two hours later, on Thanksgiving Day, Kelly Alexander issued a statement of gratitude: "We are thankful that we live in a town like Charlotte where the people understand the plight of other people, and our friends and neighbors—all over town—have showed their concern for us in the experience we have had."

Julius Chambers shared many of those sentiments, but more tentatively perhaps, for he knew that the struggle for Charlotte's soul was far from being settled. What he couldn't know, as he stared out at the rain through the broken windows of his home, was that the encounter with terror would not be his last, nor would it be an experience he would endure by himself. For a while in Charlotte, the climate of conflict would become more intense, engulfing nearly everyone who came within range, especially one of the city's most prominent white leaders, the respected federal judge who, four years later, would decide the lawsuit that Darius Swann had filed. It is safe to say that Jim McMillan's ruling in 1969, and the orders that followed over the next several years, were the most far-reaching legacy of the early discontent. With very few exceptions, Charlotte's white citizens were bewildered or enraged—betrayed, many felt, by one of their own.

II

The Struggle

3

Moving Toward a Verdict

He spent his boyhood in Robeson County—farming country in eastern North Carolina, where the wooded red clay of the piedmont plateau recedes and gently flattens into the coastal plain; where the soil turns black and sandy, stretching in a fertile arc through South Carolina and Georgia, across the south-central reaches of Alabama, then curving northward again into the Mississippi delta. For most of modern history, a pattern of racial feudalism was tied to the soil, following it westward on its sweep through the South. James B. McMillan knew the pattern well. There were places, he would later understand, where it was cruel and unforgiving—parts of South Carolina, or Mississippi and Alabama, where white people ruled with harshness and caprice. But that was not the way it was in Robeson County— not at least on the farm where McMillan was raised: a piece of land a half a mile square where eight white people, the families of his father and his uncle, tilled the land in company with the fifty or sixty blacks who lived there as well. They raised the usual staples of the black-belt South: cotton, hogs, cattle, row crops, catfish, eating what they needed, selling what they could.

The Depression came early and stayed late in that part of the South. Money was so scarce that during one particularly grim year in the early 1930s, the farm's entire yield brought two thousand dollars—a sum divided among at least fifty people. But McMillan's strongest memories are not of hard times. The thing he took with him from Robeson County, a quality that has endured in his character ever since, was a kind of elegant and deeply felt notion of civility. It was there in his demeanor as a federal judge, when the first major piece of business to pass across his desk was the lawsuit filed by Darius Swann—and when the verdict that he rendered brought threats on his life. McMillan's response was calm and stubborn, for his ruling was based on a simple understanding of the facts. Over the years, he concluded, the white officials of Charlotte and Mecklenburg County had carefully and painstakingly segregated the schools, indeed the whole society, and according to the U.S. Supreme Court, segregation was illegal. McMillan's remedy, widespread busing to achieve integration, seemed all the more radical because of its author: a soft-spoken native of the area, who had never before challenged the social order around him.

In fact, however, the ruling may have been less of a departure than it seemed, for if McMillan had never gone out of his way for the cause of civil rights, neither was he drawn to the defense of white supremacy. His first brush with integration had come at the swimming hole not far from his farmhouse—"Naked Tail Beach," he and the other children called it—where the cypress trees waded in the black-water swamps, and where little boys black and white, even a few Lumbee Indians, stripped off their clothes on the hot summer days and plunged enthusiastically into the same murky water. As far as McMillan could tell, there were no ill effects. In addition, the races coexisted peacefully on the McMillan farm: never a harsh word spoken, never a suggestion from his immediate family that whites were divinely ordained to hold the upper hand. Whites did, in fact, enjoy a position of privilege; the McMillans were gentle, cultured people who had lived in Robeson County since the eighteenth century, preserving the heritage they had brought with them from Europe: the leather-bound Gaelic Bibles and other family heirlooms, passed down carefully from one generation to the next. They had fought in the American Revolution (a few of them taking the side of the Whigs), and they had fought for the South during the War Between the States. And if they never really questioned—never openly and frontally—the racial patterns built on the ashes of slavery, they nevertheless believed in the wisdom of being kind.

Thinking back on it, Jim McMillan could see no reason why the warmth and familiarity that made paternalism benign could not survive and grow stronger in an era of equality. But such thoughts were abstractions for most of his life, after he left Robeson County for the University of North Carolina, where he did well, and moved on from there to

Harvard Law School. He graduated, entered the Navy during World War II (where his job was defusing bombs), and then moved to Charlotte to practice law. He voted against the exclusion of blacks from the North Carolina Bar Association, served on the board of the legal aid society, and made an occasional civic club speech on the slow pace of integration. Generally, however, for the first half-century of his life, he left it to others to rock the boats. He was busy with his law practice and the raising of his family—all the ordinary business of life—and it suited him fine.

Still, there was a certain ambition about him—a competitiveness and tenacity in the trial of his cases—and when a federal judgeship came open in 1968 and Senator Sam Ervin, the colorful constitutional scholar from North Carolina, asked the Mecklenburg Bar Association to recommend a replacement, McMillan was happy to be a candidate. His chief opposition was his closest friend, Joe Grier, a respected Charlotte lawyer who had been a classmate in undergraduate school at the University of North Carolina and at law school at Harvard. When McMillan first came to Charlotte, he stayed at Grier's house while he searched for a job, and both before and after their competition for the judgeship, the two men were like brothers.

McMillan was never certain why he was chosen. He had done more trial work than Grier, and thus was more visible to the members of the bar. But in the back of his mind he always wondered if there was another factor also. For the most part, Grier had been more public than McMillan in his support of integration. As chairman of the local parks and recreation commission in the early sixties, he had led the effort to desegregate the parks—a controversial step at the time it was taken—and while McMillan admired and supported Grier's accomplishment, he was spared the notoriety of having taken a stand. Whether that influenced other lawyers, he was never quite sure, but in later years, McMillan often reflected on the irony of that possibility.

In any case, he got the job, and the applause in Charlotte's legal community was nearly universal. Julius Chambers was among the well-wishers. He told his young partner, Adam Stein, that the appointment held promise. Chambers could not base his judgment on McMillan's civil rights record, which was really nonexistent. But he had served with McMillan on the board of Charlotte's newly created legal aid society, and in their occasional conversations, Chambers had been impressed with McMillan's character. The integrity was obvious. No one doubted it; nor was anyone inclined to underestimate the Presbyterian stubbornness, the quiet self-assurance that lay beneath the surface. But more than any of that, Chambers simply perceived in McMillan a kind of elemental decency, a quality that he had seen in other federal judges in the South, which often thrust them toward the center of the storm. For twenty years or more, these aristocratic white men, who were pillars of the order they were called upon to judge, had been compelled to deal with a bewildering array of constitutional questions: U.S. District Judge William Miller of Nashville, Tennessee, had ruled on the reapportionment of state legislatures, enunciating the one-man-one-vote principle that shifted the balance of political power from rural America to the nation's cities. Judge Frank Johnson, an Alabama Republican from the hill country in the northern part of the state, abolished the Alabama poll tax, ordered the desegregation of jails and prisons, and upheld the legality of the Montgomery bus boycott (the movement that thrust Martin Luther King, Jr., into the national spotlight).

But arguably at least the dean of Southern judges—the archetype for the kind of profiles in courage that became increasingly commonplace as the years unfolded—was a graying South Carolinian named J. Waties Waring. Born in 1880, after the end of Reconstruction, Waring traced his lineage through eight generations of prominent Charlestonians. He lived at 61 Meeting Street, near the Charleston harbor, in a venerable, if unimposing, townhouse built before the turn of the eighteenth century. It was only a few blocks from there to city hall, where he worked for a time as city attorney, and Waring was fond of strolling to his office in the cool of early morning, beneath the rattling palm trees and the streams of Spanish moss, with the scent of wisteria heavy in the air. It was not a setting to disturb his contentment, and for his first sixty years, Waring enjoyed a quiet life of comfortable affluence. Certainly, he never agonized over the plight of blacks. "We didn't give them any rights," he recalled years later, "but they never asked for any rights, and I didn't question it. I was raised in the atmosphere that we ought to take care of these people."

Such noblesse oblige sensibilities were offended very early during Waring's tenure on the bench. It began with a peonage dispute, a case in which a white man was accused of detaining a black and forcing him to work for almost nothing. Though many judges winked at the practice in the 1940s, Waring ordered the white man to jail. Later, he would order South Carolina's Democratic party to allow blacks to vote in statewide primaries and would require equal salaries for white and black teachers. Then, in 1948, the black citizens of Clarendon County, led by the Reverend J. A. DeLaine, went to court to secure equal schools for their children. They were tired of the inequality of expenditures—$179 a year on each white student, $43 on each black—that translated into a staggering and insulting pattern of inequity. The county refused even to build schools for blacks, and when the blacks built them for themselves, the county refused to supply heat and other utilities.

When the case came before Judge Waring, he convinced a reluctant Thurgood Marshall, the NAACP attorney who represented Clarendon County's blacks, that the time had finally come to challenge segregation head-on, even at the risk that the Supreme Court would affirm it. One of the plaintiffs in the Clarendon case, Billie S. Fleming, then a young leader in the NAACP, remembers how Judge Waring stared from the bench, a somber expression on his round, friendly face, his gray hair parted down the middle with aristocratic precision. "And he told us," says Fleming, " 'you're going down the wrong road. If you really want the courts to declare segregation to be unconstitutional, you need to draw your arguments exactly that way.' "

Marshall did, and the Supreme Court affirmed his position in 1954, to the general exultation of blacks throughout the country. Meanwhile, in Charleston, the life of J. Waties Waring was torn loose from the moorings of his first sixty years. There was at least one attempt to kill him, and the ostracism—the subtler retribution of his fellow bluebloods—became so oppressive that Waring resigned from the bench after the Supreme Court ruling, moving with his family to New York City. He returned to Charleston for the final time in 1968—to be buried in one of the city's oldest cemeteries, lowered to earth in a plain pine casket. There were three white people there, his wife, the minister, and the undertaker, and nearly three hundred blacks from all over the state, bowing their heads in a silent gesture of respect. One of those present was Billie S. Fleming, who recalled a conversation from a few years earlier: "The judge was a gentleman, never bitter about the things he went through, and one day he asked in his quiet way: He said, 'Mr. Fleming, do you really believe that I have helped your people?' I said, 'Yes sir, Judge, I do. More than any man since Abraham Lincoln.'"

While it was difficult to say for sure, Julius Chambers believed he saw similar possibilities in Jim McMillan—a similar Atticus Finch quality in his devotion to duty. It was true that people like McMillan, or Waring, or any number of their colleagues on the bench, seemed to lack the hero's lust for the noble crusade. They did not seem to need the excitement or the acclaim, or even the sense of accomplishment, that went with such efforts. But when events conspired to thrust them into controversy, when the truth and the law required a summoning of courage, they did not flinch. In any case, Chambers thought, regardless of McMillan's inclinations, the law was more clearly than ever on the side of black plaintiffs. In 1968, the Supreme Court had handed down an extremely significant ruling in *Green* v. *New Kent County*, a case from a school system in rural Virginia, where there were only two high schools, one black and one white, at opposite ends of the county. There was no particular pattern of residential segregation. White and black farms were salt-and-peppered across the landscape, and children, then as always, were bused to school to preserve a segregation that was all the more odious because it was so obviously contrived. The Fourth Circuit Court of Appeals had ruled that freedom of choice assignments were a sufficient remedy for that situation, but the Supreme Court disagreed. The New Kent County schools had an affirmative obligation, the justices declared, to eliminate the historic patterns of segregation "root and branch."

That had never happened in Charlotte, Julius Chambers argued, certainly not when the *Swann* case first went to court in 1965 and came before McMillan's predecessor, Judge Braxton Craven. Judge Craven, who had since been promoted to the court of appeals, making room for McMillan's appointment, had a general reputation as a progressive, thoughtful man, who understood the changes sweeping through his region. He regarded Julius Chambers with obvious respect, perceiving early on that he was the point man for a serious legal challenge to the segregated order. But curiously enough, Craven seemed to have little interest in the Charlotte school case. He held a brief hearing on the issue—it lasted only a day and a half—and then issued a ruling that left the plaintiffs disappointed. Charlotte, he concluded, was doing all right. There had been steady progress toward integration, and a desegregation plan, submitted to the court in 1965, met the constitutional minimum.

Julius Chambers was astonished by the ruling. During the late summer and fall of 1964, he and the other black leaders of Charlotte—chief among them Kelly Alexander, Reginald Hawkins, and Mrs. U. S. Brooks, also of the NAACP—had conducted a careful, if informal, study of the local public schools, and they had reached several disturbing conclusions. They put those conclusions in the form of a petition, signed by seventy-nine sets of black parents (including Herman Counts and Darius and Vera Swann), and they presented them to the school board on December 9. The petition charged that while there had been some undeniable improvements, much of the old pattern of dual school assignments remained in effect.

When they received no reply (except for a polite and noncommittal letter from Superintendent Craig Phillips), the blacks decided to file suit, and the original briefs that they presented on January 19, 1965, essentially echoed the points of the petition: (1) some dual school zones remained in operation, black and white school districts side by side— naked, unapologetic relics from a segregated past; (2) compounding the problem, the school board permitted transfers out of integrated schools but discouraged transfers in the opposite direction; and (3) most school faculties were completely segregated. That was the way the issue looked to Julius Chambers, and he could not imagine that the court would approve such a system.

To those on the other side, however, the reality appeared very different. Superintendent Craig Phillips, for example, had come to Charlotte in 1962, faced with a challenge that might have seemed overwhelming to a man of less confidence. Until July of 1960, there had been essentially four school systems in Charlotte and Mecklenburg County: city schools and county schools, each operating one set of schools for whites and another for blacks. Fortunately, a few visionary leaders in Charlotte, white people, as it happened, had not been at all satisfied with that particular arrangement. Most conspicuous among them was a wealthy industrialist named Oliver Rowe, patron of the arts and crusader for education, who championed the consolidation of city and county schools. It was a move that would later pave the way for successful integration, though at the time of his crusade, Rowe had other motives. Living in a wooded estate just beyond the city limits, he understood that historically, the county schools had been inferior to those in the city. Many of them had been "union" schools, serving grades one through eleven, or later one through twelve, lacking even such amenities as school libraries. The gap in quality had narrowed, Rowe knew, but the county schools were still underfunded, and more importantly, there was the strong possibility of jurisdictional disputes and pointless competition for economic resources as the growing city of Charlotte continued to stretch its boundaries.

So in the spring and the summer of 1958, Rowe began an exhausting round of speeches that took him to almost every PTA in the county. He was a forceful man, distinguished in his bearing if not quite handsome, with the bite of his opinions softened by his wit. Single-handedly at first, but later with the help of the Chamber of Commerce, he hammered away at the consolidation issue, and on June 30, 1959, the voters approved the idea in a special referendum. The actual merger took place a year later, and for the better part of two years, the schools limped along in a hybrid arrangement, with both superintendents (Elmer Garinger of the city and J. W. Wilson of the county) still on the job. In 1962 Craig Phillips replaced them, bringing in his own management team with a mandate to tame the prevailing chaos.

The task was complicated by the added burden of segregation, the habit and expensive legacy of two sets of schools, and Phillips immediately, if cautiously, began to phase in a program of nonracial zoning: school assignments based on geography, not skin color. In 1962–63, geographic zones were established for two schools. In 1963–64, twelve more schools were added to the plan, bringing the total to fourteen. By the following fall, the number had risen to forty-three, and by the summer of 1965, between the time the *Swann* case was filed and the time it first came to trial, the school system had adopted a comprehensive desegregation plan that consisted of these elements: (1) students in 99 of 109 schools were assigned entirely on the basis of geography, and the ten exceptions (all of them black) were only temporary, pending the completion of a $30 million building program; (2) freedom of choice transfers were now available to students whose parents wanted them to experience integration as well as to those who wanted to escape it; and (3) the school board committed itself to the "ultimate" elimination of segregated facilities.

School board attorney Brock Barkley had a good feeling when the hearing began on July 12, the second item on Judge Craven's docket, sandwiched between a naturalization petition and a suit against the Vick Chemical Company, the makers of cold remedies. Barkley understood that it is the mission of lawyers, particularly those involved in constitutional disputes, to develop a persuasive theory of the case, a way of understanding the law and the facts that they hope will form the basis of the judge's final ruling. Barkley's theory was simple: the Charlotte-Mecklenburg Board of Education, acting on its own, without the coercion of a federal court ruling, had made steady—indeed dramatic—progress toward eliminating the pattern of dual school assignments that had prevailed in the past. It was simply a matter of time—and not *much* time—until such assignments were ended altogether. These, Barkley argued, were not the actions of a board intent on defying the Constitution, and they did not require or merit the intrusion of the court.

Julius Chambers respected Barkley's skill, but did not concede the validity of his arguments. Among other things, he contended, the results of the board's plan had been meager at best. Out of 23,000 black students in the Charlotte-Mecklenburg system, only 2,126 (fewer than ten percent) were in school with whites, and even though more than a decade had passed since the 1954 Supreme Court decision, 66 out of Charlotte's 109 schools were entirely segregated. That was not the mark, said Chambers, of an integrated system.

Judge Craven disagreed, and by July 14, less than twenty-four hours after the hearing had ended, the judge had drafted a tersely worded ruling that accepted Brock Barkley's understanding of the case. He said the school board had shown a clear intent and had made steady progress toward ending a policy of segregated assignments. Noting the statistics that disturbed Julius Chambers, Judge Craven declared:

> The question before this court is *not* what is best for all concerned but simply what are the plaintiffs entitled to have as a matter of constitutional law. What *can* be done in a school district is different from what *must* be done. . . . As a general proposition, it is undoubtedly true that one could deliberately sit down with the purpose in mind to change [school district] lines in order to increase mixing of the races and accomplish the same with some degree of success. I know of no such duty upon either the school board or the district court. . . . I accept the testimony of Mr. David W. Harris, chairman of the board, that the zones are determined by (1) the location of the schools, and (2) housing patterns, and that this was done without regard to race.

Craven thus approved the school board's plan, with one modification: he ordered the "immediate," rather than the "ultimate," desegregation of faculty and staff.

Julius Chambers appealed the next day, filing an indignant brief charging that Judge Craven's decision was "patently erroneous." More than a year later, on October 24, 1966, the Fourth Circuit Court of Appeals upheld Craven's verdict, and the following year, Darius and Vera Swann moved away from Charlotte to resume their careers as Presbyterian missionaries. They left generally pleased with their children's education, and with their departure, it seemed that an era had come to an end. The *Swann* case was over. The courts had reached a verdict, and while substantial separation of the races still existed, there was no longer the official insult of deliberate segregation.

Still, however, the issue would not rest in the mind of Julius Chambers. How could anybody, he wondered, look at the Charlotte school system—where nearly 90 percent of black children were still in all-black schools and where that racial separation was so clearly rooted in an intricate and meticulously enforced system of law and custom dating back a hundred years—and argue that dual schools had been genuinely dismantled? So in 1968, after the Supreme Court's ruling in New Kent

County, and with the arrival of a new federal judge who might bring a fresh eye to the case, Chambers reached a bold and stubborn conclusion. The time had come, he decided, to reopen the *Swann* suit—this time, on a much grander scale.

With the help of James Nabrit of the Legal Defense Fund staff, and in consultation with such legal scholars as Tony Amsterdam of Stanford University, Chambers and his partner Adam Stein set out to document what they already knew: that the Charlotte-Mecklenburg schools were still substantially segregated, with the majority of black children—and white children, too—still in schools that were racially identifiable. Against that backdrop, and in the altered legal climate of *Green* v. *New Kent County*, Chambers and Stein sought to establish two basic points. First that continued segregation was harmful to children, reflecting itself in the atrocious test scores that prevailed in black schools, where students started out below grade level and lost ground steadily as their education progressed. ("That was important to establish," remembers Adam Stein. "You would be unlikely to get a judge terribly interested in the causes of segregation, if he didn't think it was harmful.") The second major contention in Chambers's new set of arguments was more subtle and complicated, and largely untested in other school cases. Chambers maintained that the school system's plan for geographic student assignments, which had impressed Judge Craven as an act of color blindness, was not that at all. The geographic zones had simply been *grafted* onto a pattern of segregated housing—a pattern that had been created by racial discrimination, much of which was a matter of public policy. With the help of Bob Valder of the Legal Defense Fund staff, Chambers studied segregation ordinances going back to the Civil War, and with the advice of Yale Rabin, an urban planner from Philadelphia, he documented the more recent effects of planning decisions and zoning ordinances on the concentration of blacks in certain areas of the city. He cited decisions to relocate blacks uprooted by urban renewal into all-black neighborhoods and to build all-black public housing in those same areas. In answers to interrogatories filed on March 3, 1969, Chambers put the issue this way:

With the establishment of a single set of school boundary lines in 1965, the Board engrafted school boundary lines on a racially segregated community in such a manner as to generally assign black children and white children to schools they had attended prior to the establishment of the geographic attendance zones. Since 1954, the Board has constructed 34 new elementary schools, 16 new junior high schools, and 6 new senior high schools. The Board has made additions to 63 elementary schools, 24 junior high schools and 6 senior high schools.

The location of new school facilities, the additions to existing facilities, and the school boundary lines established for these new facilities were designed to and have had the effect of perpetuating segregation in the school system.

Certainly, Chambers added, those decisions by the board did not meet the "affirmative duty" standards of New Kent County.

Even the attorneys for the school board were privately concerned about the strength and imagination of Chambers's case, and as he reviewed the law and the facts, Judge McMillan came reluctantly to the conclusion that Chambers was right. McMillan had had a long and personal involvement with the Charlotte-Mecklenburg schools. His children had attended them, and the judge himself, back in 1958, had served on the Chamber of Commerce committee on school consolidation. Until this case came before him, McMillan had shared the opinion of Judge Craven, and many of his peers in the Charlotte establishment, that the local school system was doing all right. The schools were sound academically, and far more integrated than those in other cities. In addition, McMillan had a long-standing distaste for radical remedies to the problem of segregation. Less than five years earlier, he had made a speech at the University of North Carolina, denouncing "the folly of transporting children from one school to another for the purpose of maintaining a racial balance." Nevertheless, by the end of the first set of hearings, on March 17, 1969, McMillan was convinced of what the law and the facts compelled him to do. Soon after the hearings, he went with his young law clerk, Fred Hicks, to a restaurant across the street from the federal court house, and Hicks remembers the scene this way: "We had a beer. Then he wrote out—on a napkin—all the things that he said, factually, the defendants had prevailed on. It was a long list: libraries, books, courses of study, supplies, facilities [in the predominantly black schools]. He said, 'There is no discrimination here. But let's talk about bigger issues.' The judge had read the law, and I remember he said, 'It says you have to desegregate, you have an affirmative duty, and you have to do it *now*. I don't see that there is any choice.' " So McMillan began the four-week process of crafting a ruling, one that he hoped would be gentle and persuasive, for despite the radical implications of the law, he believed that the people of Charlotte would share his reverence for it if they simply understood.

On April 23, 1969, he issued his order—twenty-one pages with unmistakable implications. "The Charlotte-Mecklenburg schools are not yet desegregated," he declared. Though progress had been made since the 1965 ruling, "approximately 14,000 of the 24,000 Negro students still attend schools that are all black, or very nearly all black, and most of the 24,000 have no white teachers. As a group Negro students score quite low on achievement tests . . . and the results are not improving under present conditions. The system of assigning pupils by 'neighborhoods,' with 'freedom of choice' for both pupils and faculty, superimposed on an urban population pattern where Negro residents have become concentrated almost entirely in one quadrant of a city of 270,000, is racially discriminatory."

McMillan cited the causes of segregated housing: private discrimination, public zoning and planning decisions, relocation due to urban renewal, the placement of public housing, and then he wrote: "Onto this . . . the 1965 school zone plan with freedom of transfer was superimposed. The Board accurately predicted that black pupils would be moved out of their midtown shotgun housing (through urban renewal) and that white residents would continue to move generally south and east. Schools were built to meet both groups. Black or nearly black schools resulted in the northwest and white or nearly all white schools resulted in the east and southeast. . . .

"Since this case was last before this court in 1965, the law (or at least the understanding of the law) has changed. School boards are now clearly charged with the affirmative duty to desegregate 'now' by positive measures. The Board is directed to submit by May 15, 1969, a positive plan . . . for effective desegregation of pupil population, to be predominantly effective in the fall of 1969 and to be completed by the fall of 1970. . . . The Board is free to consider all known ways of desegregation, including busing. . . .

"The observations in this opinion," McMillan continued, seeking to soften the impact of it, "are not intended to reflect upon the motives or the judgment of the School Board members. They have operated for four years under a court order which reflected the general understanding of 1965 about the law regarding desegregation. They have achieved a degree and volume of desegregation . . . apparently unsurpassed in these parts, and have exceeded the performance of any school board whose actions have been reviewed in appellate court decisions. The Charlotte-Mecklenburg schools in many respects are models for others. . . . [But] the rules of the game have changed, and the methods and philosophies which in good faith the Board followed are no longer adequate to complete the job which the courts now say must be done *now*. . . . The duty now appears not as simply a negative duty to refrain from active legal racial discrimination, but a duty to act positively to fashion affirmatively a school system as free as possible from the lasting effects of such historical *apartheid*. . . ."

On the subject of busing, McMillan declared: "When racial segregation was required by law, nobody evoked the neighborhood school theory to *permit* black children to attend white schools close to where they lived. The values of the theory somehow were not recognized before 1965. . . . The Board has the power to use buses for all legitimate school purposes. Buses for many years were used to operate segregated schools. There is no reason except emotion (and I confess to having felt my own share of emotion on this subject in all the years before I studied the facts) why school buses can not be used by the Board to provide the flexibility and economy necessary to desegregate the schools. . . ."

Whatever the Board's new plan to achieve integration, McMillan concluded, it should be a plan "for the effective operation of the schools in a desegregated atmosphere, removed to the greatest extent possible from entanglement with emotions, neighborhood problems, real estate values and pride. The court's task has not been easy, but it is fully realized that the task facing the Board is far more difficult and will require a conspicuous degree of further public service."

Thus McMillan sought to cajole and persuade. "He felt," remembers his clerk Fred Hicks, "that if people understood the mandate, they would see there is no choice. We are a country of *law*. McMillan is very big on the law."

So were other leaders in the Charlotte-Mecklenburg community. But there were some, including the chairman of the board of education, whose tenacity and stubbornness were nearly equal to the judge's and who were determined to contest McMillan's interpretation. In the unseasonably chilly spring of 1969, a fierce and bitter resistance took hold of the city, and the agony would not end for another five years.

4

The Resisters

Sometimes he was never quite sure why he ran for the office. Maybe it was because his mother and his sisters had all been teachers, and his father had been a high school principal in La Crosse, Virginia, and an uncle was a professor at Chapel Hill. Public education seemed to be in his blood, and there was something else also: William E. Poe felt himself drawn to the public arena. He was a man of strong will and considerable conviction, and he enjoyed the challenge and the possibilities of politics—not the glad-handing part of it, for he was never especially good at that, but he relished the confrontation with the issues of public policy. It seemed an honorable outlet for his energy and ambition, and it engaged his Harvard-trained mind far more thoroughly than the mere practice of law. Still, there were times when he had to wonder if it was worth it. Even during the days before busing was an issue—when the school system operated comfortably under Judge Craven's order and Poe was settling in to the office of school board chairman—there were black parents and white parents coming forward with demands, most of them insisting that their group was neglected, many doubting the motives of the school system's leaders. At least that was how it felt. Then suddenly, in 1968, here was Julius Chambers on the scene once again, dragging the school system back into court, and even more to the point, it seemed to Poe, lacking the decency and common courtesy to sit down with school officials and discuss the issues man-to-man.

"I never knew of any occasion when he even wrote a letter," Poe would say years later. "He never even came in and said, 'let's talk about these things.'" And then Poe added with a sudden coldness in his voice: "To some extent, it made me angry. Yeah, it sure did."

As the people of Charlotte would soon understand, Bill Poe was given to nurturing his resentments. He was certain of his judgment and his moral rectitude, and it galled him that Chambers was pointlessly adversarial, treating the school board and its chairman as people of bad faith, ignoring all their court-approved accomplishments in the field of integration. Poe had been a part of those accomplishments, supporting Superintendent Craig Phillips in the transition from overtly dual schools to geographic assignments. He had been shocked to discover, when he came on the board in 1964, that the separate schools for blacks were far from being equal. Some were still heated with potbellied stoves, and Poe helped lead the effort to change the situation. But there was a limit, he thought, to how fast you could go, and that was one of the problems in America. Black leaders, even moderates like Martin Luther King, were pushing too impatiently for radical change. In the largest sense, of course they were right. The country was rife with racial inequities, and Poe believed it was imperative for the country to change. On the other hand, he had serious misgivings about civil disobedience, much less about the riots that exploded every summer, for Poe was deeply influenced by the teachings of his father.

The elder Poe was a Southern Baptist preacher, a large, friendly man of enormous energy, who had managed a pulpit in South Hill, Virginia, while he ran the high school in nearby La Crosse. When he moved his family to Oxford, North Carolina, in the eastern part of the state, he served two rural churches five miles out of town. He cut an imposing figure before his congregations, standing six feet two inches tall and weighing two hundred pounds, with craggy features and a receding hairline, preaching an Old Testament message of upright obedience. He lacked the judgmental harshness of many fundamentalists, but for young Bill Poe, his father's message was clear, and Bill came to manhood with a deep respect for authority—divine authority first, but also the authority that was vested in government. Because of that belief, he was offended when authority was abused, and he developed a fervent distaste for the Bull Connors of the South, those radical segregationists whose fire hoses and attack dogs only made matters worse, only fueled the conviction of King and other blacks that the game was rigged and that the law itself was part of the problem. Poe was deeply disturbed by such a notion. There had been times in his own life when he had not particularly liked the implications of the law, and indeed there would be again before he left the school board. But the law was the law, and it had to be obeyed, for it was the essential prop of civilization itself.

In addition to all of that, Poe thought there were many black leaders, Julius Chambers among them, who seemed to lack a sense of realism about what was possible. They wanted what they wanted, and they wanted it now, and Poe knew the world did not work that way.

Still, whatever his annoyance with Chambers's attitude, he thought the school system's record spoke for itself, and he wasn't especially worried by the reopening of *Swann*. He had not yet read *Green* v. *New Kent County*, and even when he did, he thought the facts of the case in that rural and politically backward area of Virginia—with its pattern of integrated housing and two segregated high schools at opposite ends of the county—bore so little resemblance to the realities of Charlotte that the case wouldn't serve as much of a precedent. Still, he began to worry a little when Judge McMillan called him soon after receiving Chambers's new motion and invited him to lunch at the Charlotte City Club. The judge, friendly and informal as always, told Poe he was interested in the case, and he asked the board chairman's permission to visit a few schools. Poe voiced no objection, though he thought the request was odd. He had never quite known what to make of McMillan, had never fully trusted him the way other people seemed to. It was true that McMillan was affable enough, possessing a wit and easy charm that Poe himself might envy. But he had some screwy ideas, it seemed to Poe, a private liberalism that made people uneasy, and also an ego and ambition that were only thinly veiled by an air of humility.

It was clear during the hearings in March of 1969 that McMillan was impressed by Chambers and his arguments, and when the judge finally ruled, on April 23, Poe was stunned, if not completely surprised. Though McMillan did not specifically order busing as a remedy, he mentioned it conspicuously, and it was clear in any case that you could not eliminate racially identifiable schools in Charlotte without transporting children back and forth across the county.

Poe's first response was to telephone McMillan, and though his voice was even and his words polite, you could feel the strain and the icy tension, almost *see* the neck muscles tighten and the face turn red, as Poe struggled against the eruption of his temper. Poe was a formidable man on those occasions—tall and erect with deeply-set eyes that were sharp and intense. When he first began to speak, you almost thought there was a tremor in his voice, a rumbling somewhere beneath the glacial exterior, as if the ice might crack and the rage beneath it might rush through the opening. But it didn't this time, and he simply told McMillan: "Jim, I have read your opinion and I really have trouble believing that you've done this. You are new to the bench, and I just wonder if you want to start your career this way."

McMillan replied, with no hesitation and no apparent animosity, that he had made a careful study of the law and the facts, and yes, this was what he wanted to do.

From that moment on, the battle was joined. Poe was convinced, and said repeatedly, that McMillan's order would be the ruin of the system. He simply didn't believe that the white people of Charlotte would allow busing to occur—particularly not those in the affluent southeastern section of the city, where the oak trees spread across the narrow, winding lanes, or farther out, where the open farm lands of a decade ago were rapidly being filled by the sprawl of new development.

In a string of civic-club meetings beginning May 1, 1969, Poe declared himself "unequivocally" opposed to busing, charging that Southern school systems had been "singled out" by the courts to bear the burden of social change. "I am not committed," he said, "to the proposition that we are going to move people—by force of law—to provide what some sociologist feels is the ideal social climate."

When the school board met on May 2 at Charlotte's public television station, WTVI, Poe was greeted by an emotional crowd of fifty parents, who had descended on the studio. "We're getting a feeling of complete frustration that has been building up over the years," one father told the board. "We're beginning to feel like we're being pushed around." Another parent warned, speaking with a bluster that came from the heart: "I don't think there's anything more important in the world to us than our children. When you start messing with our children, brother, you've had it."

Poe listened carefully, fidgeting occasionally as the speakers began to repeat themselves, but seeking nevertheless to offer reassurance: "There are a few of us on the board," he said, "who feel like you do."

Thus Poe set the tone and the direction of his early leadership. He soon became the key figure in the legal resistance, and having chosen that road, he found thousands of Charlotteans who were eager to follow. But there was a problem with that. While Poe was determined to fight the issue in the courts, there were others more activist—some of good will, some less so—whose protests pushed the community toward the edge of violence.

Tom Harris remembers the night he first got involved. He didn't mean to. He had never been any kind of an activist, had never even voted, in fact, since 1955. But he arrived home from work on April 29, not quite a week after McMillan's first ruling, and his wife informed him there was a meeting that night, a few neighbors getting together to talk about the schools. When Harris arrived, there were about a dozen other people, and they spoke fervently about the implications of what the judge had ordered. Harris liked what he heard. None of the others seemed to be segregationists. They felt, as he did, that it was not a racial issue—that the presence of blacks in school with their children was not a problem worth discussing. But the idea that a U.S. District Judge—an official beyond the power of the people to elect—could uproot their children and bus them across the city, sending them into neighborhoods that were far away and alien, well, that was an outrage, a notion so preposterous that you would almost laugh if the judge didn't seem to be so serious about it.

All of them agreed it was essential to resist, and they picked Tom Harris as their leader and spokesman. It was an unaccustomed role for him, though in retrospect, there was wisdom in the choice. Harris cut quite a figure at six-feet-two and two hundred pounds—not much more than his playing weight as a Duke linebacker in the 1940s—and though he was only forty-one, his hair had begun to turn a distinguished-looking silver. He was also an affable and forceful man, but more than that, as his neighbors would tell you, there was something fundamentally decent about him—an air of *fairness* in which he took great pride. Though his job was selling insurance, and later real estate, his avocation was refereeing football games—a calling that appealed in an elemental way. There was nothing exact or scientific about it, but you studied the rules and called the game as you saw it and took responsibility for the decisions that you made. That was a pretty good formula for life, as Harris saw it, and he tried to let it guide him through the frantic months ahead.

He called a meeting for the following Friday night, May 2, and when he arrived at Quail Hollow Junior High School, a collection of flat brick buildings flanked by a ball field carved from old pastures, he couldn't believe what he saw. "The people were coming across those fields like Genghis Khan," he remembered years later. There were so many, in fact, that they quickly filled up the Quail Hollow gym and had to meet in two sessions. Harris told them essentially the same thing that he had said Tuesday night—that the issue was not racial, nor was it a matter of desegregation. Separate but equal schools had never been equal, and that was wrong. It was not, however, a wrong to be corrected at the expense of their freedom, and it was their God-given right and duty to resist.

Harris and the other leaders circulated a petition that had been drafted for them by Charlotte attorney Robert Potter. It was precise and rather moderate in its legalese, calling on the school board to submit a pupil assignment plan in response to McMillan's order that would "retain the freedom of any student to attend the school of his choice, and further to provide a system of bus transportation at taxpayers' expense for any student who requests transfer out of a school where his race is in the majority to any school where his race is in a minority. . . . We further urge you to impress upon the court the undesirable disruption to the living pattern of all citizens which would result from requiring any student on a daily basis to be bused or otherwise transported to a school several miles from his home." If such pleas, coupled with some changes in school district boundaries aimed at furthering integration, did not satisfy Judge McMillan, then the petition declared: "We the undersigned citizens and taxpayers request you to enter an appeal from such decision of the district court."

By Sunday night, forty-eight hours later, the petition had been signed by 10,738 people. Harris was amazed by the total, and yet he could feel it coming at the Friday night meeting. The intensity of the gathering was almost startling, and when the second session finally ended, he and a few others who had emerged as leaders went back to his house. It was a handsome structure, brick and two stories, nestled serenely on an oak-shaded lot, surrounded by the homes of people like himself, barely half a mile from his young daughter's school. Yes, they agreed, it was crazy to uproot young children from a setting like that, sending them to ghetto neighborhoods where they were certain to be unwelcome, if not in serious danger. The parents talked enthusiastically of the emerging resistance.

One of those at the house that night was an impressive Charlotte doctor by the name of Don Roberson. He was intense and intelligent, with an ascerbic sense of humor, and although Harris had never met him before, he sensed in Roberson a compatible commitment and devotion to the cause. It wasn't long before the doctor was sharing the podium with him—sharply dressed in his houndstooth jacket, peering at the crowd through his dark-rimmed glasses, as he told them with conviction: "I don't see how the schools can open under an order that requires mass busing. The people don't want it, and a lot of the ones I've talked to won't do it."

They called their organization the Concerned Parents Association (CPA), and as its following swelled into the tens of thousands, they addressed rally after rally in Mecklenburg County, traveled to other cities to encourage similar groups, and several times flew to Washington to harangue the noncommittal aides to President Richard Nixon. On one of those trips, they presented Nixon's adviser George Shultz with a petition containing 67,355 signatures—more than a fourth of the population of Charlotte.

Harris had to admit that those were heady times. And yet somehow there was a dark side to them, for he recognized that things were on the edge of being out of hand. Already, there had been two thousand angry picketers at the federal courthouse, some of them hanging Judge Mc-Millan in effigy, and even worse than that, for several nights in a row there had been smaller crowds at the judge's house. Harris didn't approve of such things. There was little in his nature that was nasty or violent, and he feared that the political climate in Charlotte might become some of both.

"As you got wrapped up in it all," he remembered much later, "sometimes you'd go home at night and it's dark and you're alone, and you say, 'how would I feel if one of those silly boycotts got started and something unfortunate happened?' I'd say, 'hell, that would be terrible.' You can start off innocent, but flat get out of hand. It was an inflammatory thing, man. If you're part and parcel to anything like that, you may have to answer to your conscience some pretty tough questions."

Harris was a man who took his conscience seriously, and the time would soon come when he would face some hard questions. Like Bill Poe, he would have to ask himself whether his goal was to serve the public schools—whether he would join the fight to save them—or whether he would sacrifice them on the altar of his own ideology. In 1969 and 1970, however, that was a decision for the future. For now, he was determined to turn things around, and the way to do that, he thought, was for the CPA to join the system, to elect some of its members to the Charlotte school board.

Jane Scott never liked campaigning. It was hard for her to approach a group of people she didn't know, stick out her hand and say, "Please vote for me." It offended her sense of reserve, a deeply held feeling of privacy and propriety that was so much a part of her personality. The speeches, though, were a different matter. They gave her an opportunity to speak her mind on the issue of busing, and that was one subject that needed strong words. Her husband, Jack Scott, had said it many times at CPA rallies: Busing was an outrageous usurpation of freedom. But in Jane Scott's view it was more than that. It was also a senseless distraction, well intentioned perhaps, but destructive nevertheless, from the real educational issues in Mecklenburg County. It was true that black children—and white children, too—were not getting the kind of education they deserved. But the problem, she thought, was not the racial composition of classrooms, nor could it be solved by shaking up children like dice in a jar and scattering them helter-skelter to new schools around the county.

In fact, Mrs. Scott thought, it was racist to tell black children that the only way they could get a decent education was to be in a minority in every school in the system. Jane herself was the product of integrated schools. She had graduated from Germantown High School in Pennsylvania, which was so heavily black it was in danger of tipping, and her middle child was in Paw Creek Elementary, which had been naturally desegregated for the last several years. She saw no problem with any of that. But it was a terrible thing to uproot children from their neighborhood schools and bus them across town to schools where they were certain to feel out of place—all in the misguided notion that it would improve their education. It wouldn't, of course. It would simply drain the school system's energy and resources from the more critical task of getting back to the basics.

"You can't improve education by moving people around," she liked to say. And that was why, in March of 1970, she had agreed to join Tom Harris and a CPA lawyer named Bill Booe in running for the school board. She had wanted her husband to do it. For months, now, Jack Scott had been one of the CPA's most impassioned speakers. But he was also a doctor, a general practitioner in the nearby town of Mt. Holly, and the demands of his practice were simply too heavy. So Jane had decided to run, and she was glad of it now. It was important for her part of town to be represented.

The Scotts lived in the West Side of Charlotte, an area very different from the silk-stocking suburbs in the distant southeast, where Tom Harris and his neighbors had formed the CPA. The West Side was a hodgepodge. It consisted partly of old mill villages, with their simple frame houses and rambling brick factories, long since absorbed by the city of Charlotte. There were vast housing projects on West Boulevard, an officially contrived population of poor blacks that had helped convince Julius Chambers and Judge McMillan that Charlotte's residential segregation was not a matter of chance. Interspersed with all of that, out beyond the factories and the interstate highways, were the newer subdivisions that were far more prosperous. Jane and Jack Scott lived in one of these, an area of ranch houses and carefully trimmed lawns, but even the West Siders who had a little money often tended to feel isolated and neglected.

Nearly every public official in Charlotte, elected or appointed, came from the affluent southeastern quadrant of the city, and thus it came as no surprise to the Scotts that when Judge McMillan handed down his first decision in 1969, and when the school board developed a desegregation plan in response, the West Side was chosen as the sacrificial lamb. The board had decided to pair Paw Creek Elementary with the abandoned, formerly all-black Woodland Elementary, sending grades one through four to Paw Creek, busing the fifth and sixth grades to Woodland, and perhaps most incredibly, running both schools with only one principal.

"I was angry as the dickens," Mrs. Scott remembers. "Incensed is a very nice way to put it. Outraged is probably closer. I felt we had to do something to stop it." So they canvassed the neighborhood door-to-door, and after marshaling popular support, filed a lawsuit. Later, on at least two occasions, they heard that school officials were on the way to Paw Creek to remove its mobile classrooms, which were no longer needed after the pairing with Woodland. In response, the Scotts and their neighbors organized hundreds of parents into a human chain around the school, gathering on one occasion at one o'clock in the morning. Out of such defiance, which the Scotts like to compare to the Boston Tea Party, grew a strong West Side antibusing organization—a group called, coincidentally, the Concerned Parents Association, which soon merged with Tom Harris's organization of the same name.

Harris was pleased by the West Side's involvement. He was glad to see his organization develop a citywide following, and when it began to focus its efforts on the school board election, Harris saw Jane Scott as an excellent candidate. She was intelligent, articulate, and at the age of thirty-three, she was very attractive in a prim sort of way. She had high cheekbones, finely chiseled features, and long blond hair that she usually wore in a bun. Moreover, her knowledge of education (her mother and father had both been teachers) tended to provide the CPA with an added touch of respectability and class.

Bill Booe also fit the mood of the times. He was a maverick Republican from the Charlotte right wing, regarded by some as a segregationist at heart. He was a ferocious spokesman for the antibusing cause, and the only question in the minds of his allies was whether or not he would prove *too* ferocious. It was true in a sense that he was a man of principle. But opposition of any kind, even on questions of strategy, often drove him into a rage. His face would turn red and his bearing adversarial, like a Golden Gloves boxer suddenly trapped in a corner, or a working-class Perry Mason who would just as soon do his fighting in the streets. He threatened lawsuits and attacked people's motives, and during a discussion of his legal fees for the CPA, he and Tom Harris once nearly came to blows. But there was also, on occasion, a certain eager friendliness about him, or if not quite that, at least a deep yearning for people to like him. And in any case, during the school board election of 1970, the primary object of Bill Booe's rage was the hated court decree of Jim McMillan, a priority that put him squarely in sync with most of Charlotte's citizens.

He would often campaign with Jane Scott and Tom Harris, and frequently with a school board incumbent named Sam McNinch—an insurance salesman, slow talking and earnest, who delivered at almost every stop what reporters used to call his "pall mall to socialism speech." Meanwhile, their supporters built an intricate and effective precinct organization, and when the voting was over, there was cause for elation in the CPA. Tom Harris and Bill Booe were elected outright, Harris with 20,066 votes and Booe with 18,760. Gone from the school board were its respected but rather colorless vice-chairman, Ben Huntley, and Betsey Kelly, a smart, abrasive, Northern-bred proponent of integration who managed to gather only 7,000 votes. Jane Scott ran third, and found herself in a runoff with the board's only black. She won, but even for some people in the CPA it was hard to take much elation in the defeat of Coleman Kerry, a Baptist minister who had the dignity and bearing of a youngish grandfather—genteel, articulate, with an easy smile and a gentle sense of humor that were valuable resources for an embittered school board.

The CPA victory was hollow in another way, too. It seemed to change very little. Judge McMillan proved impervious to the public outcry, rejecting every plan for pupil assignment that did not involve busing, and though legal appeals of his rulings had been set in motion, they had yet to bring results. So in the months between the 1970 election and the beginning of school the following September, community frustration grew steadily more intense. At a CPA rally in February, Jack Scott had already called for a "mass boycott" of the schools, and that form of protest, more drastic than petitions, lawsuits, or a run for the school board, became the CPA's next goal. The leaders acknowledged the gravity of the step. "We are coming into a time of individual decision," Don Roberson declared at one meeting. "The fellow next to you can't make it. Your neighbor can't make it. I can't make it, and Tom Harris can't make it. You must weigh it heavily, thoughtfully, prayerfully."

As the summer neared its end, the CPA called on the school board not to open classes, and at an organizational rally on August 27, an emotional Baptist minister named Jack Hudson, pastor of what was then the largest church in Charlotte, recalled the New Testament martyrdom of John the Baptist. Invoking the inspiration of that biblical example, and comparing it to the mission of the antibusing movement, Reverend Hudson proclaimed: "I would to God it could be said here tonight, there are people in the CPA who are willing to lose their heads because they are in the right."

5

The Buses Must Roll

That was the climate in which Bill Self had to function, and he found it painful. Self was the superintendent of the Charlotte-Mecklenburg system, having succeeded Craig Phillips in 1967, and he wanted to see an accommodation between the school system and the courts, one that took account of the moral and legal imperatives identified by Judge McMillan, as well as the administrative realities confronting the schools. Self knew that finding such a balance was no easy task. The school board majority, under the guidance of Bill Poe, was determined not to give in to the judge, and whatever the board's latent instincts for moderation and compromise, those were now buried beneath an avalanche of protest.

In Self's estimation, that was a tragedy. He believed in the rightness of racial integration, understood the old deceits of separate but equal. He had been involved with the issue since the 1950s, first in Winston-Salem and then in Charlotte; and as Craig Phillips's top assistant in both of those cities, he had been proud of the progress they were able to make. Self was an administrator by temperament and training. He was avuncular and balding, with a strength and a poise that served him well under pressure, and an active conscience that helped shape his decisions. Still, despite his undisputed competence and the respect and affection of most of those who knew him, he was never really certain he was the man for the job—not in Charlotte in the 1970s, where the climate of strife, he said, was "a little rich for my blood."

Good administrators, he believed, faced either inward or outward: they were either very skilled at dealing with the public—at setting goals and giving them voice in a way that engendered broad support—or they were more private people, able to sit down around a table and build a quiet consensus about how to solve a problem. Craig Phillips had always been a *public* superintendent, smart and forceful, with an air of great charm, able to deal effectively with the community at large. Self, meanwhile, was more comfortable facing inward, tending to the schools on an everyday basis—a skill that was useful in ordinary times, but strained by a crisis that required a public role.

Phillips, however, was gone from the scene—moving on in 1967 to become a foundation executive, and later state superintendent of schools—and as the obvious choice to replace him, Self was determined to give it his best. If he had any doubts about the delicacy of the challenge, they had quickly been erased on the night of May 2, 1969, when the school board met at WTVI. Judge McMillan's order was nine days old, the Concerned Parents were meeting at Quail Hollow Junior High, and before the evening was over, more than fifty of them would descend on the board meeting to register their protests. Bill Poe, too, had made his feelings clear, and though Self held the board chairman in highest regard, and though he felt sympathy of sorts for the protesting parents, he thought it was important to speak his own mind. He said that he believed the court ruling was a moral, as well as a legal issue; that he had supported desegregation for all of his career; and that it was important to obey the law as the courts understood it.

Bill Poe was shocked at such heresy, for the implication seemed to be that the board ought to do what McMillan was demanding. When the meeting ended, he led Self into a room adjoining the studio where the board had convened, and with the flush of anger rising in his face, he said the superintendent's comments had been out of place—that Self could change his attitude, in fact, or find a new job. When word of the exchange finally trickled out to the press, both men sought to deny or downplay it. They understood that the media's recounting of a moment of friction—even an accurate recounting—had a way of casting hard feelings into stone, and they knew they still had to work with each other. But the superintendent reported the incident to trusted members of his staff—Chris Folk, Bob Hanes, John Phillips, and others—seeking to underscore the difficulty of their task. They had been thrust into the role of brokers or diplomats—middle men, whose job was to devise a pupil assignment plan that the court would approve and the board would accept. It was no easy undertaking, Self acknowledged. But the survival of the school system demanded that they try.

"I wasn't stupid," says Self. "I knew that geographic zoning could not completely desegregate the schools. You could still find all-black and all-white. Any thinking person knew you had to break away—sever the umbilical between school and residence. And that, of course, meant busing."

One late spring day after McMillan had ruled, Self and two of his assistants, Chris Folk and John Phillips, were on their way to Greensboro for an administrators conference. As they made their way up Interstate 85, Self began to talk about the different possibilities. It was a complicated issue, he said. But he had been thinking about an approach that he thought held promise, even though it would mean a great deal of busing. He said children in a given neighborhood ought to be assigned to a particular elementary school, or perhaps to a pair of elementary schools, one for the lower grades, another for the years just before junior high. Then all children in those elementaries would be assigned to the same junior high; and all those in a given junior high would go to the same high school. If that could be done, Self mused, if children—even those bused out of their neighborhoods—could form friendships that they *knew* would last for all twelve grades, perhaps they would adjust more easily to the change.

Folk and Phillips thought the idea was a good one. They had no way of foreseeing, of course, that with modifications it would represent the core of the "Feeder Plan" for desegregation that would emerge in Charlotte after years of legal wrangling. Indeed, in the early days, they knew it was not even something they could propose to the board, for Bill Poe and a slim five-member majority were determined to hang on to neighborhood schools. Still, Self thought it was important to delineate the options, and he set to work with his staff to define what they were. They would gather in a corner conference room down the hall from Self's office, a kind of hideaway with three large maps on the wall, and a fourth-floor window overlooking the skyline. As the months unfolded, they came up with nineteen different alternatives, ranging from the kind of freedom of choice arrangement that had failed in the past to an intricate busing plan not far from the one that Judge McMillan would eventually order.

Self was efficient and meticulous throughout the process. Surrounded by his charts and his maps, he looked every inch the school superintendent. He was tall and gray haired, with an angular face and, often as not, a dark business suit and a pair of dark-rimmed glasses. He spoke so softly that people were sometimes inclined to take him for granted. But he also possessed a reassuring calmness—a patience that served him well in the heat of those times and won him the affection of the members of his staff. There was a *fineness* about him, Chris Folk thought, and almost to a man the other assistants agreed. But Self had his critics also—people who thought he wasn't forceful enough in leading the school board—and probably there was truth in that assessment. For the most part, Self *didn't* try to lead them, to persuade the board members of his own point of view, for they, not he, were supposed to set policy. But he did try to *guide* them. He wanted to see them make decisions on the basis of the facts, even when the facts were not especially pleasant.

"I felt," Self now remembers from the safety of retirement, "like a student presenting a paper to a very critical teacher. The paper would come back, and in the margins it would say, 'you did good on this, this and this, but bad on that. Go back and try again.' "

The problem with Self's analogy, as he will quickly tell you, is that there were actually two teachers, the school board and the district court, each grading his efforts by entirely different standards. From the summer of 1969 through the first eight months of 1970, there were a half-dozen major court rulings and school board responses, with no obvious result except the deepening of a standoff. For Self, the anxiety of the process took a terrible toll, and late in the evening, or on the weekends, the superintendent sought relief in an odd little hobby: he was a bricklayer, working hard on a patio in the yard behind his house, listening most times to the gentle, wistful harmonies of Simon and Garfunkel. More and more, in fact, as the months went by, Self looked forward to giving up his job, thought with satisfaction about a time in the future when he could put all the tensions behind him for good. But in the troubled spring of 1969, during the weeks immediately following McMillan's first ruling, he knew that that time had not yet arrived.

McMillan had great sympathy for the superintendent. He always saw him as a remarkably good man, and he knew from reading the newspaper that the desegregation plan submitted by the school board on May 28, 1969, was a watered-down version of what Self had proposed. The board's plan, in fact, changed almost nothing. It redrew the boundaries of a few school zones, promised free bus transportation for majority to minority pupil transfers, asked for volunteers to desegregate the faculties, and promised generally to employ other measures if enough volunteers did not step forward. The plan also called for the closing of formerly black Second Ward High School, which was located squarely in the heart of downtown, and was therefore, in McMillan's view, the easiest high school in the system to desegregate. Meanwhile, the board proposal left the majority of black students in all-black schools.

The plan sparked an immediate outcry in Charlotte's black community. One leader, Reginald Hawkins, noted bitterly that Bill Poe's own children would have attended Second Ward if the school had been integrated, and he called for the board chairman to give up his job. Julius Chambers, meanwhile, filed an indignant brief urging Judge McMillan to declare the board in contempt. Its plan, he said, did not accomplish—did not even *pretend* to accomplish—what McMillan had ordered, which was the elimination of segregated schools. The Supreme Court had made it plain in *Green* v. *New Kent County* that white schools and black schools were no longer acceptable, and McMillan had ruled quite correctly that the standard applied to Charlotte-Mecklenburg. But the school board had defiantly refused to accept that standard, relying instead on the same basic practices that had perpetuated segregation.

McMillan agreed with that assessment, but in a June 16 order, he declined to hold the board in contempt, hoping instead to persuade and cajole them into compliance. "The members of the board," he wrote, "have had uncomplimentary things to say about each other and about the court, and many of them obviously disagree with the legality and propriety of the order of the court." But such sentiments, he continued, could be regarded as *disagreement*, rather than contempt. Indeed, said

McMillan, he himself was "not far removed from active participation in the time-honored custom of criticizing a judge who has ruled against him. Moreover," he added, "on an issue of such significance, the amount of foot-dragging which has taken place, up to now at least, should not be considered as contempt of court."

Nonetheless, McMillan said the board's attitudes and proposals needed to change, and change right away. He noted with approval the efforts of Bill Self to guide the board in formulating a plan. "No express guidelines were given the superintendent," he wrote. "However, the views of many [school board] members . . . were so opposed to serious and substantial desegregation that everyone including the superintendent could reasonably have concluded, as the court does, that a 'minimal' plan was what was called for, and that the 'plan' was essentially a prelude to anticipated disapproval and appeal. In a county criss-crossed by school bus routes for 23,000 pupils, more than twenty thousand citizens, mostly from affluent suburbia, many of whose children undoubtedly go to school on school buses, signed petitions against 'involuntary' busing of students. The frenzy of parents received a ready forum in televised meetings of the board. The staff were never directed to do any serious work on re-drawing of school zone lines, pairing of schools, combining zones, grouping of schools . . . nor any other possible methods of making real progress towards desegregation.

"The superintendent," McMillan continued, "revealed the general terms of his plan within a few days and later presented it formally on May 8, 1969. It provided for full faculty desegregation in 1969, which the superintendent said he considered feasible. It provided moderate changes in the pupil assignment plans; and it contemplated future study of the other methods of desegregation suggested in the April 23, 1969, order.

"The board then met, struck out virtually all the effective provisions of the superintendent's plan, and asked for more time from the court." None of that would do, McMillan said. The board was directed to submit a new plan by August 4.

Bill Poe knew it was necessary to give up some ground, but he was determined to do it slowly and grudgingly, seeking to preserve the concept of neighborhood schools. Not everyone on the school board agreed with that approach, and two adversaries stood out from the rest. Carlton Watkins was a Charlotte pediatrician, good-humored and frumpy, with thinning hair that always seemed tousled, and a kind of pent-up drive that probably contributed to a heart attack in 1971. He recovered fairly quickly, and remained on the board, but in the wake of that scare, he felt compelled to slow his pace. There would be fewer stolen lunch hours and late nights at home, poring over city maps and stacks of census data, trying to devise his own plan for desegregation. Dr. Watkins grieved—that is not too strong a word—over the plight of his city. He hated the standoff, increasingly intransigent, between the school board and the federal court, hated the mounting conflicts among the members of the board, and perhaps most of all, hated to see the frenzy of the community at large. He thought that maybe the CPA rallies and the crowds of bitter parents haranguing the board would all go away, if only he could come up with a plan that would integrate every school, thus satisfying the judge, and minimize busing, thus soothing the fears of the people of Charlotte. He came very close. He grouped the seventy-two elementary schools into eighteen clusters, or districts, of several schools each. Fourteen of the eighteen districts were composed of schools in contiguous areas. The remaining four clusters involved some degree of crosstown busing, but less than other alternatives that were being considered. Though the plan had its rough spots, Watkins was convinced it could work.

He was supported in his efforts—at least in the spirit of them—by Betsey Kelly and Coleman Kerry, while they remained on the board, and perhaps most importantly by a middle-aged widow named Julia Maulden, who may have been the board's most respected member. "I don't know anybody who wants to do *right* more than Julia Maulden," Bill Poe would acknowledge years later. And that assessment was borne out by the story of her life. After her time on the board, she joined the Peace Corps and became a teacher in Zaire, coordinated an economic development project in Haiti, and in 1986, went to Nicaragua with a religious peace group, hoping that the presence of Americans near the Honduran border would help deter attacks by guerrillas in the area. She was a woman of strong and quite stubborn principle. At the heart of her ethic was her Presbyterian Christianity, which compelled her to make common cause with the world's underdogs. Thus, if black children in Charlotte were enduring the deprivations of segregated schools, there was no moral alternative to the pursuit of integration. Still, the voice of her faith also whispered a caution: it warned her of the dangers of excessive self-righteousness and led her to value civility in the midst of disagreement. Though she disapproved strongly of Bill Poe's priorities, and of the occasional petulance that she thought was beneath him, she also sought to be respectful in her scoldings. Once she told him sternly in a private moment of exasperation: "If you had one *ounce* of humility, you would be the perfect man." But if Mrs. Maulden had a gift for candor that somehow did not offend, hers remained a voice in the wilderness. She favored a creative compliance with Judge McMillan's order, and during the troubled months of 1969 and 1970, she simply didn't have the votes. Nor did her friend, Carlton Watkins.

Bill Poe did, however, and he was determined to guide the school system on what he regarded as a solid middle course. He was uneasy about the militance of the CPA, particularly in 1970 when the organization's efforts turned toward a boycott, and he didn't mind stepping up the level of desegregation. But he was determined to preserve the integrity of neighborhood schools, and as a result, the school board's second attempt at compliance with Judge McMillan's order, submitted July 29, was not a lot different from the plan of May 28. It rejected pairing, clusters, and all forms of busing, and left some twelve thousand students in schools that were nearly all black. For the first time, however, it did acknowledge the school board's affirmative duty to desegregate, and it closed seven black schools, reassigning those students, along with 1,245 others, to formerly white schools. It also committed the board and the school system's staff to a thorough study of further methods to achieve integration.

Reluctantly, McMillan approved the plan for the fall of 1969, but he ordered the board to submit a new proposal for 1970—one that would make "full use of zoning, pairing, grouping, clustering, transportation and other techniques . . . having in mind as its goal for 1970–71 the complete desegregation of the entire system." He wanted, he said, no more racially identifiable schools. "In *Green* v. *New Kent County*

School Board . . . the Supreme Court held that school boards have the *affirmative duty* to get rid of dual school systems, to eliminate 'black schools' and 'white schools,' and to operate 'just schools.' . . . The issue," he continued, "is one of law and order. Unless and until the Constitution is amended, it is and will be unlawful to operate segregated public schools. . . . *The question is not whether people like desegregated public schools, but what the law requires of those who operate them.*"

In McMillan's mind, he could scarcely have been more emphatic or specific, so he was astonished when the school system's lawyers (Brock Barkley, William Waggoner, and Ben Horack) filed a brief in October that declared: "The Board of Education does not feel that it will be possible to produce pupil desegregation in each school by September 1970." Then, on November 17, the board submitted its newest plan for desegregation, which left thousands of students in white or black schools, and also proclaimed: "A majority of the board believes that the Constitutional requirements for desegregation will be achieved by the restructuring of attendance lines, the restricting of freedom of transfer and other provisions of this plan. The majority of the board has, therefore, discarded further consideration of pairing, grouping, clustering or transporting."

Already, Julius Chambers and other attorneys for the plaintiffs had become annoyed at what they regarded as McMillan's excessive patience with the school board. "On three different occasions," they declared in a November brief, "this Court has urged, encouraged and requested the defendant School Board to carry out its constitutional duty to desegregate the Charlotte-Mecklenburg public schools. The Court has literally leaned over backwards to seek voluntary compliance by the Board. . . . Despite these efforts, however, the Board now unequivocally, defiantly and contumaciously advises the Court that it will not now, nor in the future, carry out its constitutional responsibilities."

McMillan agreed, and in a forceful new order on December 1, his patience seemed to snap. "The board has, in seven months, failed to produce a program for desegregation," he wrote. And he recited once again the figures on racially identifiable schools, the dismal test scores of blacks who remained segregated, and the constitutional mandate as he understood it. Then he quoted at length from the words of Felix Frankfurter, the late Supreme Court justice who had written in the case of *Cooper* v. *Aaron* in 1958: "The responsibility of those who exercise power in a democratic government is not to reflect inflamed public feeling, but to help form its understanding. . . . Lincoln's appeal to 'the better angels of our nature' failed to avert a fratricidal war. But the compassionate wisdom of Lincoln's First and Second Inaugurals bequeathed to the Union, cemented in blood, a moral heritage which, when drawn upon in times of stress and strife, is sure to find specific ways and means to surmount difficulties that may appear to be insurmountable."

In McMillan's mind, the unanswered question was whether the board would finally choose to draw on that noble heritage, or whether it would continue its disgraceful stonewalling. He still hoped Bill Poe and the others would choose the former option, but in the meantime he appointed a consultant, Dr. John Finger of Rhode Island College, to prepare a plan for total integration. The goal, he said, but not the absolute requirement, was for every school in Charlotte-Mecklenburg to reflect the 71:29 ratio of whites to blacks in the system as a whole. The plan was due in early February, and the next two months were a busy time for Bill Self and his staff. They had been instructed by the court to assist Dr. Finger, and they took the mandate seriously. They gave him an office not far from Self's, just up the hall from the fourth-floor corner where the superintendent and the others were developing their own alternatives for achieving integration. They found Dr. Finger a soft-spoken, tactful, and cooperative man, who relied heavily on the thinking of the staff in his hasty formulation of a plan for the court.

Meanwhile, the staff continued its work with the school board majority, trying once again to come up with a plan that would satisfy McMillan, while preserving the concept of neighborhood schools.

Complicating the task was the additional pressure of a new Supreme Court decision from the previous fall. On October 29, 1969, the court had grown tired of the resistance and the stalling by school officials in Holmes County, Mississippi, and had ordered those schools integrated "at once," in the middle of the first semester. Citing that precedent, Julius Chambers's partner Adam Stein, who had worked intermittently on the *Swann* case from the beginning (along with Conrad Pearson, Jack Greenberg, and others), drafted a motion on January 19, 1970, asking that Dr. Finger's plan be submitted to the court right away—and that it be *implemented* no later than January 26.

Judge McMillan didn't feel bound by Adam Stein's deadline. But the plaintiff's motion, and the Supreme Court ruling on which it was based, underscored a sense of urgency that the judge himself was beginning to feel. Thus, when the school board came forward with its newest proposal, which changed the boundaries of school zones but left ten schools identifiably black and another twenty-five more than ninety percent white, McMillan chose the Finger Plan, with its haphazard patterns of large-scale busing. On February 5, 1970, he ordered it implemented that same school year.

The members of the school board, he wrote, "after four opportunities and nearly ten months of time, have failed to submit a lawful plan (one that desegregates all the schools). This default on their part leaves the court in the position of being forced to prepare or choose a lawful plan."

McMillan still encouraged the school board to come up with something better; the issue was not the plan but the results, he said, and the result he had in mind was the elimination of racially identifiable schools. More specifically, the board was forbidden to operate any predominantly black schools, and was instructed to make "efforts" to reach a 71:29 white to black ratio in every school. In addition, in what may have been the most unsettling portion of his order, McMillan accepted the precedent of *Alexander* v. *Holmes* and ordered that his ruling be implemented that same school year. Elementary school students, he said, should be reassigned by April 1, and junior high and high school reassignments should be accomplished no later than the fourth day of May.

It was then that an enraged school board decided to appeal, leaving the whole community in a state of tense waiting. The Concerned Parents Association stepped up its protests, and within a few weeks, Tom Harris, Jane Scott, and Bill Booe were running for the school board.

It was a time of great strain for Judge McMillan. Already, there had been angry crowds outside his house, and threats on his life too numerous to count, and sinister phone calls late in the night. And even the

First Presbyterian Church in downtown Charlotte—with its wrought-iron fences and its familiar stone walls and the other reassuring reminders of his Presbyterian certainty—had become a chillier place these days. Once-friendly faces were now stiffly polite, and though the judge accepted the ostracism with grace, he was stung by the change. Those who knew him say his faith didn't falter—his long-term conviction that life was unfolding as it should—and McMillan himself once told a reporter: "The way I figure it, you have to assume God has a plan for your life. You do your best to understand what it is, then you try not to depart from it too far." But in the short run, such Christian resignation could not erase the anxiety, nor could it subdue entirely the seething anger inherent in a stubborn test of wills. It was McMillan v. Poe, the Fatalistic Presbyterian v. the Upright Baptist, and those who knew both men were startled sometimes by the degree to which each of them had personalized the issue. Yes, they were each propelled into battle by the demands of their principles—McMillan by his understanding of the U.S. Constitution, Poe by his fear for the destruction of the schools. But it was also true that they intended to *win*, and thus the contest grew more intense: The school board pursued its appeal and the CPA stepped up its protests, and McMillan held firm with few apparent allies.

It was about this time that Adam Stein remembers noticing a recurring little twitch around McMillan's eye—tiny and involuntary—and he remembers thinking that he hadn't seen that before. He wondered if the judge had begun to fear a reversal, a blunt repudiation from a higher court that would fan the flames of an irate community and ensure the finality of McMillan's isolation. Stein knew for a fact that such a thing was possible. Along with other attorneys for the plaintiffs, he had been the recipient of an icy bit of warning from Judge Braxton Craven, McMillan's predecessor and the judge before whom the *Swann* case had first come to court. Craven was now a member of the Fourth Circuit Court of Appeals, which would soon pass judgment on McMillan's rulings, and in a conference with the lawyers Craven had indicated that the judgment would not be favorable. As Adam Stein remembers it, he told them quite coldly: "You guys have led your friend McMillan out on a limb. And we're about to cut it off behind him."

The prediction proved true. Because of his prior involvement in the case, Craven excused himself from the Fourth Circuit's consideration of it, but in a badly divided opinion, the remaining judges vacated a part of McMillan's decision. They directed him to hold new hearings and apply a "test of reasonableness" to the extensive busing of elementary students. The plaintiffs appealed, and McMillan held the hearings. Then on August 7, 1970, in a move that revealed the depths of his certainty and stubbornness, he ruled that his February decision had been reasonable. He ordered it reinstated when school opened in the fall.

The school board asked Chief Justice Warren Burger for a stay in the implementation of the order (a stay of execution, some antibusing people liked to call it), but on August 25, to the widespread shock of the people of Charlotte, Justice Burger refused. The high court, he said, would hear the case in October, but in the meantime, it was the duty of the school system to obey the district court. The buses would roll in September.

So with a sense of foreboding and the helpless realization that it was all happening too fast, Bill Self and his staff made hasty plans for the opening of school. Self still believed, or hoped at least, that in the long run the school system would find itself strengthened. But he feared that the short run was going to be tense, and he braced himself for the ugliest first week of classes since 1957, when Dorothy Counts had been admitted to Harding High School.

As he looked back on it later, Self realized that he had been right. His long-term hopes and his short-term fears were squarely on target.

6

Hitting Bottom

After a couple of weeks, the bomb scares were routine. Chris Folk, however, remembers the first one vividly: It came about 7:00 A.M., only a few minutes after he arrived at his office. He had left his house at about 6:40, and covered the five miles to downtown in maybe ten or twelve minutes—winding his way through an old Charlotte neighborhood, where the oak branches met to form a canopy across the road, and the early morning sun filtered softly through the leaves. The day was pretty with the first hint of fall, but Folk was a little jumpy. In the first place, Chris Jr., who was six and the oldest of his three young children, was about to begin his first day in school, and like any conscientious father, Folk couldn't help but feel a bit of apprehension. But there were other things more heavily on his mind. It was September 9, 1970, the opening day of school in Charlotte-Mecklenburg, when 525 school buses, 191 more than the year before, were already beginning their routes across the county.

Folk was a veteran school administrator, one of Bill Self's most trusted assistants, and he knew that busing was nothing new in Charlotte. For decades, in fact—almost since the invention of the bus—it had been a primary tool for preserving segregation. Now, however, that purpose had been turned on its end, and the city was tense with the anticipation of trouble. In a strong appeal to the public, Bill Poe had urged the community to "put aside personal feelings and join with the Board of Education in attempting to make the best of the situation that confronts us." But at the Education Center, they had made elaborate plans to handle problems if they came.

A corner office overlooking downtown, the same room, in fact, where Self and his staff had spent endless hours mapping plans for integration, had been transformed into what they now called "the war room." They had named it that in a moment of grim humor, but during the first weeks of school in 1970, the name seemed to fit. The room contained a couple of conference tables and a bank of telephones, designed to assure rapid communication with any school in the system. Scheduled to handle the phones were the superintendent himself, always a calming influence, along with the school system's director of security, Roland Smith, the chiefs of police for both the city and the county, and Self's three top aides, Chris Folk, John Phillips, and Robert Hanes.

On September 9, the first phone rang almost at exactly 7:00, and Folk was astonished to discover that it was his wife. Slightly shaken, she told him that an anonymous caller only a few minutes before had informed her that a bomb had been planted at their house. "Get your children out," the caller had warned. The police quickly made a search of the house, found nothing, and at least for the moment, Chris Folk relaxed. "What a first day for Chris Jr.," he thought. And then the bomb scares resumed: 8:10, South Mecklenburg High School; 10:04, South Mecklenburg again, leading to an early dismissal of the school; 10:40, Quail Hollow Junior High; 10:42, Elizabeth Elementary; 1:40 P.M., Merry Oaks Elementary. In all, there were six that day, and more the next, and they were to continue, in fact, throughout the semester. After a while, nobody believed them, and yet you never knew. They were still unsettling, cowardly, and sinister, and they added something ugly to the tension and the gloom.

But there were other, more serious problems commanding the staff's attention. Already, the opening of classes had been delayed for nine days, as officials worked frantically on last-minute preparations. They were reassigning children, making repairs (it was necessary, they had to admit, to spruce up the black schools for the arrival of whites), and installing new books and furniture in the paired elementaries. In addition, they also embarked on a hurried search for buses, borrowing approximately two hundred well-worn specimens, which they nicknamed "old soldiers," from other parts of the state.

They knew that the Concerned Parents Association had proclaimed a boycott, and they were chagrined to discover that it was effective.

White enrollment was sharply down, and even after the boycott ran its course, an estimated three thousand five hundred white students were lost immediately to private schools. Indeed, in the first five years of busing, private school enrollment more than tripled in Mecklenburg County, and estimates of white flight ran as high as ten thousand students.

Meanwhile, the level of community tension seemed, if anything, to grow worse with time. School board meetings were regularly besieged by angry crowds of white parents, railing against the tyranny of the federal court system, the cowardice of the school board for giving in to it. And there were also some scattered acts of terrorism—a word that didn't seem too strong to the victims. Among the first was John Phillips, the wise and steady assistant superintendent of schools, a man of soft-spoken wit and steadfast commitment to the pursuit of integration. Phillips lived not far from Chris Folk, in a neighborhood straight from the canvas of Norman Rockwell, with suburban brick houses, healthy-looking lawns, and stands of maple trees changing color in the fall. It was not a place for night riders, but one morning Phillips was awakened by the sounds of shattered glass, followed immediately by his young daughter's screams. It was right around two o'clock, and as he bolted toward her room, he heard a squeal of tires and the roar of an engine, and then he saw the terror on her face. Shards of glass were everywhere, and he found a rock on the other side of the room. It was large enough to be lethal, and as he surveyed the damage, Phillips realized that it had not only crushed the window above his daughter's bed, but had hit the wall across the room with such force that it had broken through the slats behind the plaster.

For Phillips and his family, the months after that were an anxious time. Every sound in the night, every random backfire from a passing automobile, seemed to carry with it the promise of danger. He had to wonder, sometimes, what he had done to attract their attention. Maybe, he thought, they had figured out that he favored integration, and if that was the crime, they had the right man. Phillips had grown up outside of Newton, North Carolina, in the rolling farm country just east of the Appalachians. He often saw the buses hauling black children to school on the other side of the county, always passing white schools along the way, but in those days, he says, you didn't think about it much; that was simply how it was. Phillips, however, began his introspections on the issue of race during artillery training in World War II. "I went to Fort Sill, Oklahoma, and it was the first time I had been thrown in with blacks, who were certainly equal and capable, and some sharper than I. You looked at it, and you wondered." Then Phillips went to work in public education, and his experience under Craig Phillips, who was no relation, and later under Bill Self had deepened his sensitivity to the issue. Indeed, he had spent many professional hours wrestling with the dilemmas that integration presented, and he expected that in the end, the schools and society would be the better for it. Integration was morally right and educationally sound, and if his fear was the temporary price of that conviction, well, so be it.

Phillips also knew—and it was a source of grim comfort—that he was in less danger than other players in the drama; less, certainly, than Judge McMillan, who was under constant threat, or Julius Chambers, who was the most frequent target of the night riders' revenge. Chambers had enjoyed a break of five years from the bombing of his home in 1965, or the earlier explosion that ripped through his car while he was speaking at a rally in the town of New Bern. But as the buses began to roll in 1970, and as the *Swann* case made its way to the Supreme Court, the attacks resumed. And the maddening thing was that the first two were indirect: they were aimed, not at Chambers himself, but at his father, whose repair garage in Mt. Gilead, North Carolina, was burned in August, and then again on New Year's Day. After that, the stoicism came almost easily when Chambers received an early morning phone call, on February 4, 1971. It was his wife, Vivian, and she told him that once again she had bad news. His Charlotte law office had been the target of arson, and the damage was heavy—maybe fifty thousand dollars' worth, the police would later estimate. Chambers was staying at a Raleigh motel, and he thought of driving back right away, but it was 4:30 in the morning, and the roads were frozen, and what difference would it make if he were there anyway? So he fixed himself a drink and went back to sleep.

Chambers was heartened, however, when he returned to Charlotte and saw the response of the city's legal and religious community.

Several dozen volunteers, many of them from the wealthiest churches in the city, turned out to scrape paint and clean floors in a temporary office building donated to the firm. Several thousand dollars came in in contributions, and lawyers who had opposed Chambers in the courtroom made copies of their own files available, replacing those he had lost in the fire.

Violence was not Charlotte's style, the city's leadership declared. But in fact, the attack on Chambers was not the worst of it. The most horrifying moments occurred in the schools, and the official records are grim and cryptic: October 20, 1970, West Mecklenburg High School—six blacks rob a white boy at knife point; December 1, West Charlotte High—a white boy draws a pistol on a group of black students. Such are the notations in the school system's files. But the memories are much more vivid than that. For John Phillips and others who lived through the times, there are searing images that will never go away: of a kind of violence more frightening somehow—more *personal* and full of hate—than what they had endured during World War II. Phillips remembers a particular episode at Harding High School, where the mobs had threatened Dorothy Counts in 1957. He hadn't been in Charlotte back then. But Harding in the seventies seemed far more tense. There were lines of policemen with gas masks and batons, and armed Klansmen milling just beyond the school grounds, and crowds of black students with chains and two-by-fours. "Bob Hanes and I were there," Phillips says, "and we were talking to the lieutenant in charge, and he said it looked like the whites were going to make a charge. The police put on their masks, and Bob and I didn't have one. I thought, 'I've been through the war; what in the hell am I doing in this kind of place?' " At that point, Phillips was swept up in a kind of elemental horror—a fear not just for himself, though that was part of it, but also for the city and the schools, and indeed for the country. Several things seemed clear in a moment such as that: The mob of white people was just as ugly as any from the fifties; their hatred and their epithets just as disturbing. But the change, of course, was on the other side of the police line, where the black students chanted and brandished their weapons. These, Phillips thought, were not the dignified heirs to Dorothy Counts, Gus Roberts, or the other pioneers of 1957. They had not come to school in freshly starched shirts or prim checkered dresses, nor did they carry themselves with patient self-containment. These were angry people: young men and women, who had come of age when militancy was exploding into cries for black power, and the sermons of nonviolence—the words that had stirred their parents' generation—seemed pale and irrelevant. "I've been to the mountaintop, and I've seen the promised land." Many of these young people still remembered the speech, but they also knew what had happened next—how a bullet fired from a high-powered rifle had torn through the face of Martin Luther King—and, as far as they were concerned, nonviolence itself had died on the balcony.

In addition to all of that, there were other factors to compound the alienation of the young blacks of Charlotte. There were the long bus rides to school every morning, and at the end of the ride they were always a minority, isolated, unwelcome—or at least that was how it felt—and their anger grew stronger as the weeks went by. "We were thirteen miles from home," remembers Dexter Feaster, who was bused across town from his housing project to Independence High School. "When classes were over, they could get in their cars and go home. We didn't have any cars. We had to mill around and wait for the buses."

Feaster was a good-looking kid in those days, tall and muscular and superbly athletic, a wide receiver on the football team. He got his diploma and then his college degree, and after several years in professional football, he is now a coach in the Charlotte-Mecklenburg system. Looking back, he says he believes in the value of integrated schools. They improved the educational opportunities for blacks, and dramatized for all students, black and white, the need to coexist in a world full of differences. But it was a lesson learned on the other side of trouble, for in the early days of busing, the collective chip on the black students' shoulders represented an easy provocation for a great many whites, who were still working through their own prejudice, inflamed for the moment by the examples of their parents. It was a volatile mix that exploded again and again at every upper-grade school in the system. Even junior high schools were not immune, but the worst uprisings came among the older students. Between 1970 and the early spring of 1973, race riots had closed nine of the ten high schools in the Charlotte-

Mecklenburg system, forcing most to suspend classes for several days at a time.

The lone exception was Independence, where Dexter Feaster was a football star, and where the principal—a soft-spoken white man by the name of Sam Haywood—worked, obsessively almost, to assure that the cataclysm did not come. Haywood knew he was defying the odds, but he thought he might pull it off. Independence was a new school, built in 1967, and it had been integrated from the very beginning. The staff was strong, with black teachers like Esther Hargrave and whites like Dale Borneman, and Haywood encouraged them to be visible in their friendships: to talk openly with each other in the lobby before school, to sit together in the school cafeteria, to bear witness, in short, to the ideal of integration. Race was a chasm that it was possible to bridge, and Haywood wanted the students to know it. He organized workshops in human relations, and he relied from time to time on corny little gimmicks (ice cream was a penny if you bought a cone for a person of another race). But more than anything else, Haywood relied on himself. He was a hardworking man, only thirty-four years old when he came to Independence, and a little enigmatic, many people thought. He seemed quiet and moody sometimes, with eyes that first struck you as large and sad. But there was also a friendliness about him, a certain self-bemusement that made him seem approachable. Most students liked and trusted him. "I thought he cared a lot," says Dexter Feaster. "He was a compassionate man."

But in the end, however, none of that was enough, for during the lunch hour of March 7, 1973, blacks and whites squared off on an Independence patio, and somebody threw a two-by-four through a plate-glass window. Haywood heard that it was Dexter Feaster, and he immediately despaired. Feaster was one that you would expect to be a peacemaker. He was smart and popular, and he generally seemed to have his head on straight. Later, Feaster denied that he had broken the window. He said he had tried to rescue a white friend from a group of blacks, and then another group of white boys had jumped him. "A window was broken," he said, "but I didn't do it." Whatever happened, the campus was soon aswarm with crowds of blacks and whites, yelling, threatening, tearing at each other's hair, some of them hitting with whatever they could find. The police arrived quickly, and though most of them performed their duties with efficiency and restraint, there were scattered and inevitable allegations of brutality. The fighting grew worse before it dissipated, and as Haywood and his faculty tried to pull students apart, they occasionally found themselves the targets of punches. There were dozens of injuries, most not serious, and then it ended, leaving Haywood to ponder the damages.

He went to his office, and there in the shadows of late afternoon, he began to write a letter to the students—a group of people whom only a few days before he had regarded as a family. "Dear Students:" he began. "I don't know how to start this letter except to say something you know already. Trouble has come to our school. . . ." He paused in the writing, his thoughts suddenly lost in a jumble of emotion. They had been so angry, so vicious towards each other, and the image came again of the twisted young faces. Had he failed? Was there more he could have done? Or were the times so terrible that nothing was enough? The letter, he decided, could wait for awhile. For now, in the privacy and the deepening gloom of his sparsely furnished office, Haywood put his head on the desk—and quietly wept.

Bill Poe could understand the feeling. Crying wasn't his style, but nobody felt the pain of those years more acutely. It was exactly the kind of agony he had always feared, the inevitable consequence of such a radical change. Why couldn't Judge McMillan see that? What kind of pride could cause such oblivion? Still, once the disruption and upheavals had spread to the schools, Poe tried to resist the lure of demagoguery. I-told-you-sos accomplished nothing, he thought. The crisis was upon them, and it was up to the leaders to pull the school system through. He adopted a tone of firm moderation, trying to appeal to the community's best instincts. Nothing was solved by violence, he said, nor could it be allowed.

At the same time, however, Poe was determined to relieve the city of its anguish, to remove the foolish burden that McMillan had imposed. He was deeply involved in the school board's appeal, pursuing the legal fight to the U.S. Supreme Court. Poe felt pretty good about the school system's chances. He thought their case had a lot to recommend it, and he had a great deal of confidence in the school board's lawyers. Brock Barkley had become old and tired, but he had been assisted for some time now by young Bill Waggoner, hardworking and determined—a bit shy, perhaps, and maybe a little awed by the magnitude of the task; he was, after all, a small-town boy from Salisbury, North Carolina, pleasant and balding, the son of a Salisbury lawyer. He had some good help. Since the summer of 1969, he had worked in tandem with Ben Horack, who, in Poe's estimation, was one of Charlotte's best attorneys.

Horack had been on the school board in 1957. He was one of the seven white men who had voted, despite the frequent threats on their lives, to admit Dorothy Counts to Harding High School, Gus Roberts to Central, and two other black students to white junior high schools. He regarded the moment as the proudest of his life, not because he had suddenly seen the light and become a crusader against segregation, but simply because he had vowed to do his duty. Horack was a self-confident man of homespun eloquence, the son of the dean of the Duke law school. He had been raised with a reverence for the law, and as Brock Barkley had explained it to the school board in 1957, the obligations of the Constitution were now crystal clear. The *Brown* decision had outlawed segregation, and the question now was whether you believed in law and order or whether you didn't.

All of that gave Horack a certain passion for his work. He was offended by the notion that Charlotte had failed to do its duty, and when Bill Poe called him on a Sunday afternoon, seeking reinforcements in the struggle with McMillan, Horack felt a personal investment in the task. Charlotte, he believed, had set the pace for the nation, and the progress hadn't stopped in 1957. So he threw himself into the task of assisting Bill Waggoner, and the two of them worked very well together. It was exhilarating, really—the sixteen-hour days, the feeling that they were David in the fight against Goliath. The civil rights wave was surging toward a crest, but in Horack's view, it had become entirely too powerful. The things that Julius Chambers was seeking, and that Judge McMillan seemed willing to grant, were simply not reasonable. The Fourth Circuit Court of Appeals seemed to offer some hope of relief when it remanded the case to McMillan for further consideration, but the judge had reinstated his original order. Clearly, relief would have to come from a higher authority.

As the summer of 1970 came to an end, Horack and Waggoner began preparing for the Supreme Court hearing set for October. They were optimistic about their chances. They had contacted lawyers involved in school desegregation suits all over the country, including New Kent County, Virginia, which had been cited as a precedent in the Charlotte case. "I'm guilty," the New Kent lawyer had said to Bill Waggoner, and he went on to explain that in New Kent County, they had resisted desegregation as hard as they could. That was obviously not the situation in Charlotte. From 1957 until the city ran afoul of Judge McMillan, it had done everything that the courts had required, and more. Surely, the Supreme Court justices could understand that, especially now that the liberal Earl Warren had retired, and Warren Burger had replaced him. Burger was a man with a solid reputation, and he even looked the part of a thoughtful chief justice, white haired and scholarly, with wise and friendly eyes and, from the bench at least, an air of self-possession.

But if Horack and the others felt strongly about their case, morally as well as legally, and if they had grown hopeful that the Supreme Court would pay attention, they were also aware—vaguely at first, and acutely later on—that things were not exactly falling into place. First, Bill Poe and Horack had led a delegation to Washington to seek the help of a prominent lawyer by the name of Charles Rhyne, a former resident of Mecklenburg County, who later became president of the American Bar Association and an attorney for President Nixon. They asked Rhyne to handle the Supreme Court arguments, believing that his experience and prestige would enhance Charlotte's chances. Rhyne, however, had turned them down. His schedule was crowded, he said, and there was not enough time to prepare. He suggested that they go to his friend and colleague in Richmond, Lewis Powell. But the Charlotte delegation was not yet familiar with Powell's reputation, and though some of them later second-guessed the decision, kicking themselves after Powell was appointed to the U.S. Supreme Court, they decided to try a different approach. Poe made a second trip to Washington, accompanied this time by Bill Self, and they paid a visit to Ervin Griswold, the solicitor general of the United States. Poe respected Griswold, who had been one of his law professors at Harvard, and he thought it would help if the Nixon administration was officially staked out on the side of Charlotte-Mecklenburg. Griswold agreed to enter the case, and Poe was pleased. Horack and Waggoner—"the local boys," as Waggoner liked to call them—could argue before the court with greater assurance and credibility, now that the U.S. government had declared its support.

As the weeks went by, however, it became clear that the solicitor general didn't have the time or inclination to come to Charlotte and work in close association with the school board's attorneys. And when the case was finally argued, on October 12, 1970, Griswold's presentation seemed vague and abstract, disturbingly out of sync with what Horack and Waggoner were trying to accomplish. At one point in the proceedings, Justice John Harlan demanded of Griswold, "Did Judge McMillan abuse his discretion?"

"That depends on what Judge McMillan had in mind," said Griswold, and he went on to say that if McMillan had intended the total elimination of black schools, then yes, he had gone too far; and if he had in mind racial balance, that too went beyond the constitutional mandate. But if McMillan was merely seeking to disestablish dual schools, then the remedy might *not* be an abuse of discretion. To the Charlotte people, such arguments sounded fuzzy and uncertain. Had McMillan gone too far, or had he not?

Nor were things any better when Waggoner or Horack tried to make the case. Neither man had been to the Supreme Court before, and it was an intimidating environment the first time around—the justices there above you behind the great wooden bench, elevated so high that all you could see were their heads and their black-robed shoulders, and occasionally, if it was Justice Hugo Black, a crooked, bony finger, pointing at you fiercely every time he asked a question. It was not that Waggoner and Horack were frightened by that. They were capable men, and there was simply no question about their level of preparation. They could cite chapter and verse from a stack of legal opinions more than three feet high, and they knew quite well what they wanted to say. The problem was the *format*—the justices' irritating habit of interrupting with questions, derailing your argument before you could even make it.

The Charlotte attorneys had planned for Waggoner to open on the subject of racial balance, with Horack to follow with the case against busing. But when the bombardment of questions began, the neat division was lost, as Justice Thurgood Marshall demanded: "Mr. Waggoner, do you have any children of tender age riding school buses as of 1969?"

"Well, not of tender age," Waggoner replied, looking puzzled.

"I don't mean you personally, but the Charlotte school system. They were busing children of tender age, weren't they?"

"They were busing children of tender age."

"For the purpose of maintaining segregation?"

"No, sir."

"For what other reason?"

"They were bused to get them to school . . ."

". . . Did they ever pass a colored school on the way?" Marshall persisted. ". . . I am talking about before this plan went into effect, when you did have colored schools and white schools."

Marshall looked far less vigorous than he had twenty years earlier, when he had been the chief counsel for the NAACP and had argued the *Brown* case with such effectiveness. His health had become intermittently bad, and he seemed tired sometimes. But Waggoner had to give him credit for tenacity.

". . . We bused white children past black schools, and black children past white schools," Waggoner conceded. "This is incontrovertible . . ."

"So what is wrong with busing them for the purpose of integrating?"

"Do two wrongs make a right?" Waggoner asked.

"Is that the only answer?"

"I think so, yes, sir."

That was how it went as the minutes dragged on, with Bill Poe watching glumly from the spectators' gallery. It wasn't that Waggoner's answers were bad, and he and Horack were holding on to their poise. But they just weren't able to control the discussion, to guide its direction and to make the firm case that Charlotte, North Carolina—far from needing to apologize for its civil rights record—had been a national leader in the move to desegregate.

Julius Chambers, meanwhile, was absolutely unflappable; brilliant, some observers thought, as if he had rehearsed his answers before he ever came in the room—which in fact he had. The week before, the NAACP Legal Defense Fund had staged mock hearings at Howard University and then at Columbia, with panels of prominent lawyers playing the role of the justices. Chambers had not been very good at the first rehearsal. His answers were choppy, and he seemed off stride. And though he had been better at Columbia, his partner, Adam Stein, was still a little worried. But on the day of the hearing, Chambers was icy. He knew what he wanted to say, and with the quiet intensity that was becoming his trademark, he went about the business of getting it in the record. The issue, he said, was whether the school board could perpetuate identifiably black schools that had been "created and fostered by state action. . . . The extensive segregation in this system was not fortuitous," he continued. It was the result of geographic assignments grafted onto a pattern of segregated housing, which had been created substantially by actions of the state: zoning ordinances, planning decisions, urban renewal, the location of public housing. Under the standards of *Green* v. *New Kent County*, there had to be a change. Segregation in the schools must be eliminated, root and branch.

"Black children and parents in Charlotte have struggled since *Brown*," Chambers argued. ". . . They desired desegregated education, and know that it can only be obtained under a plan like the one directed by the District Court below. It would be a rejection of a faith that black children and parents have had in *Brown*, the hope of eventually obtaining a desegregated education, for this Court now to reverse the decision of the District Court and now adopt, sixteen years after *Brown*, a test that would sanction the continued operation of racially segregated schools."

At his best, Chambers could be eloquent, and curiously enough, the thing that gave his arguments their force was that he did not speak with any obvious emotion. His voice was flat, almost a monotone, and he rarely displayed any frustration or anger. But you got the feeling after listening for awhile, that on some buried level he was angry all the time, and held it in check with impeccable self-restraint. Whatever, Chambers, at 34, was obviously a young lawyer who argued with conviction.

He was backed at the *Swann* hearings by the intelligence of James Nabrit, an attorney from the staff of the NAACP Legal Defense Fund, who had worked on the case with Chambers, Adam Stein, Conrad Pearson, and others. Before the Supreme Court, Nabrit, if anything, was more elegant than Chambers—taller, more polished in his bearing, as he sought to make the point that contrary to the arguments of the school board's attorneys, Judge McMillan had not imposed a standard of arbitrary racial balance (the percentage of black students had varied widely from school to school), but McMillan had, quite properly, ordered the elimination of every vestige of official segregation. There were to be no black schools, no white schools; "just schools," as the court had put it so succinctly in *Green*.

As the hearings came to an end, Bill Poe was worried. He didn't think the school system had made its best case. Chambers, meanwhile, was quietly optimistic. He didn't see how they could have done any better.

The justices gathered to discuss the matter right away, on October 17, 1970, the Saturday after the two-day hearing. They could all agree that *Swann* was important, maybe even a landmark on the order of *Brown*. In retrospect, the wisdom and courage of the 1954 decision were obvious: even school board attorneys invoked its precedent, and as movingly as any single event in recent American history, it had focused attention on the nation's great dilemma. But what now? There had been other desegregation rulings in sixteen years, and taken together, they represented a steady march in the direction of equal justice, a fulfillment of the promise of the U.S. Constitution. None of the justices wanted to see a retreat. But to some of them at least, the *Swann* case was different. If busing were affirmed, or racial balance, or the importance of housing patterns that were partly state induced, then suddenly integration was not a Southern issue. The great urban ghettos in the industrial Northeast, the barrios of Denver, Los Angeles, and Austin, were immediately open targets for wrenching social change. Justice Burger worried about the potential for chaos, and Justice Hugo Black—the old Alabamian who had long been a stalwart of the court's liberal wing—saw busing also as the place to draw the line. Where, he asked his clerks, does the Constitution use the word?

Burger and Black, however, were in a minority. John Harlan, William Brennan, Thurgood Marshall, and William O. Douglas were all determined to see the court affirm McMillan, and even the moderates seemed inclined in that direction. Potter Stewart, frequently the swing man on the Warren Court, who played the same role under Chief Justice Burger, had been especially impressed with McMillan's courage, and with the persuasive quality of the district court opinions. Stewart had looked up the judge's name in a recent *Who's Who* and, as he later explained to legal scholars and reporters, was surprised to discover he and McMillan were about the same age. Stewart had been at Yale while McMillan was at Harvard, and both were Navy men. He wanted to do right by the district court judge, and in next six months, he played a key role in the difficult task of forging a consensus. The ruling that resulted, on April 20, 1971, addressed five major issues: The first was whether racial quotas, or targets, were a matter of constitutional right, or whether they were *required* as a remedy for past segregation. The court said no, they were neither a right nor a necessary remedy, but could be *permitted* because McMillan had used them only as "a starting point." The second question was whether one-race schools were *necessarily* forbidden, and again the court ruled that they were not. But, said the justices, where there had been a history of segregation, there was also "a presumption against schools that are substantially disproportionate in their racial composition"—and McMillan's elimination of such schools in Charlotte had been within his discretion.

The next two questions were related. The first was whether schools could be paired or clustered, and attendance lines gerrymandered, in the pursuit of integration. Absolutely, said the justices. "The remedy for . . . segregation may be administratively awkward, inconvenient, and even bizarre in some situations. . . . [But] when school authorities present a district court with a 'loaded game board,' affirmative action in the form of remedial altering of attendance zones is proper. . . . The pairing and grouping of noncontiguous school zones" was also acceptable. And was it permissible for a judge to order the busing of students from one noncontiguous zone to another? Yes, said the justices. Such "remedial techniques" were within the court's power.

But what of the future? What were the responsibilities of a school board once segregation had been eliminated "root and branch," as the court had once put it? What if changing population patterns caused a "natural" process of resegregation? Were courts or school authorities required to stop it? In a victory for the court's more conservative members, the justices said no. "Neither school authorities nor district courts are constitutionally *required* to make year-by-year adjustments of the racial composition of student bodies once the affirmative duty to desegregate has been accomplished and racial discrimination through official action has been eliminated from the system." But—and this would become important later for Charlotte—school authorities *could* make adjustments if they wanted to, and in fact, could even institute the kind of rigid racial balance that courts were forbidden to order. As the justices explained it: "School authorities are traditionally charged with broad power to formulate and implement educational policy and might well conclude, for example, that in order to prepare students to live in a pluralistic society each school should have a prescribed ratio of Negro to white students reflecting the proportion for the district as a whole. To do this as an educational policy is within the broad discretionary powers of school authorities."

So there it was. For constitutional scholars, there was a little something for everyone: for the conservatives, no flat prohibition of one-race schools, no judicially imposed requirement for a fixed racial balance, no guarantees against resegregation; and for the liberals, an approval of busing and other related techniques—the only tools that made metropolitan integration really feasible—and an affirmation once again that while deliberate segregation was absolutely forbidden, deliberate integration was not. Those issues were important in the nation as a whole. In Charlotte, however, what mattered most was the court's bottom line—literally, the last sentence of the ruling: "The order of the district court . . . is affirmed."

Bill Poe was devastated. He had pursued a legal fight that he had expected to win, a cause that he passionately believed was right, but now he had lost, and that fact presented him with a bitter dilemma. The highest court in the land had issued its decree, and if he believed in the law—if he prided himself on respecting its authority, particularly at a time when disobedience was rampant and the whole country seemed to be losing its head—there was nothing to do but accept the court's judgment. Still, it seemed so wrong, so foolish, so needlessly disruptive, and that was the issue he had to wrestle with. Even some of his opponents would soon come to admire the honesty of his struggle, and after Poe had resolved it and taken his stand, they were even more impressed with the result. Over the next several years, said Julia Maulden, a member of the school board's liberal minority, "Bill Poe displayed a manfulness and integrity of character seldom seen in public life." But that was in the future. For now, the board chairman was simply depressed.

Jim McMillan, of course, responded very differently. If anything, his personal stake was much higher than Poe's. His life had been repeatedly threatened, and even among his fellow citizens too civilized for that, he had become a pariah. He was patient about it, and undeniably brave, but McMillan was also an affable man—charming and gregarious when he put his mind to it, a person accustomed to the respect of his peers. He had been willing to risk all that on the notion that he was right, but if the highest court had ruled otherwise, well, that was not even something he wanted to think about. So he struggled with his poise when the ruling came down, trying to keep his emotions from showing too much. But he permitted himself a little satisfied smile, or maybe the emotion was simply relief; then he turned to one of his law clerks and said, "I got it right, didn't I."

7

A Slow Change of Mood

From the beginning, there were people who thought so, though in the first several years they were a small and lonely group: a preacher here and there with a protest sign, an editor writing sermons in the morning newspaper. But there were precious few others who stepped forward to agree.

Gene Owens, however, didn't mind the lonesome role. He was an iconoclast at heart, a large, friendly man, with hair turning white though he was only thirty-nine, and a rich baritone voice that always sounded like he was speaking from a pulpit—which, in fact, he often was. Owens was the new minister at Myers Park Baptist Church, and he had to admit it was a daunting position. Myers Park was a wealthy congregation, perhaps the most prestigious in Charlotte. It had opened its doors in the 1940s, founded by a group of prominent citizens that included Fred Helms, Jim McMillan's law partner before he ascended to the bench, and a dozen other men of early middle age—intelligent, thoughtful, and caught up in a concern that weighed heavily on their minds. Their children, they felt, were straying from religion—or at least from the restrictiveness of the Baptist religion—and the founders began planning for a different kind of church: a place of beauty and reverence that would never be described as narrow, indifferent, repressive, or petty—adjectives, they had to agree, that were correctly applied to many Baptists in the South.

Their first minister had been a gentle-spirited pastor named George Heaton. But the character of Myers Park Baptist jelled most completely around Heaton's successor, a tall, stoop-shouldered, pipe-smoking preacher named Carlyle Marney. An outspoken liberal in the fifties and sixties, Marney took delight in shaking up the flock, combining eloquent sermons and a needling sense of humor to challenge complacency wherever he found it. Marney was proud of the Myers Park church, and particularly so when its influential members applied Christianity in the rest of their lives—when, for example, a Myers Park deacon and Chamber of Commerce leader named Ed Burnside played a leading role, in 1963, in the voluntary desegregation of Charlotte's lunch counters. But if Marney believed that Christianity should not be confined within the walls of a church, he himself was eloquent on Sundays, reveling in the sound of his own forceful voice and dazzling the people with the poetry of his thoughts. *Time* magazine called him one of the world's outstanding theologians, and when he stepped aside with heart problems, submitting his resignation on Good Friday, 1967, Gene Owens was left with a tough act to follow.

He knew, however, that he was suited to the task. He understood the character and importance of Southern religion, and like Carlyle Marney, he had long been drawn to the Old Testament prophets, those wonderful iconoclasts like Amos and Micah, Isaiah and Jeremiah, who always seemed at odds with the social order around them, and who spoke in an imagery that had to stir your soul—"Justice cascading like a mighty river." That was the tradition that had to be kept alive, and the opportunity was there to nurture it in Charlotte.

Owens had arrived in the city in January of 1969, only a few months before McMillan's first ruling, and he understood immediately the implications of the issue. Antibusing leaders Don Roberson and Tom Harris were both members of his church—Roberson quite active, Harris less so—and though neither had agreed with Carlyle Marney, they were proud to be a part of Myers Park Baptist. Owens liked them personally, but he winced at the rhetoric of the CPA, believing that despite the protestations of Harris and other leaders, the issue of race was at the core of the struggle. As he surveyed the moral landscape, Owens felt himself torn away from the most visible Baptists: Harris, Don Roberson, or the more moderate Bill Poe, who spent his Sundays at First Baptist only a few miles away. He was drawn instead to Jim McMillan, for he felt (it was many years later before he could articulate it neatly) that McMillan was a modern heir to the prophetic tradition. Buoyed, apparently, by his Presbyterian fatalism, the judge was clinging stubbornly to a loftier understanding, reminding the community of a higher moral calling.

"We are called to do justly, to love mercy," says Owens. "It's a decision that has been made for us. I think Jim held us to it. He saw something in this community that Bill Poe didn't. He said, 'we are better than that. Or by God, we ought to be.' "

It wasn't that Owens had contempt for Bill Poe. He understood—or at least he later came to see—that Poe was motivated by deep principles of his own. He was committed to the strength and survival of the Charlotte-Mecklenburg schools, and he genuinely feared their destruction in the wake of McMillan's orders. But if Poe had realistic fears about the dangers of the moment, he lacked McMillan's ability to peer into the future—to see the potential in a time that had not yet arrived. In the final analysis, Poe's view of human nature was too constricted, too pessimistic, somehow, while even at the time, McMillan's seemed to contain just a touch of nobility.

So Owens looked for ways to demonstrate his support. Joined by Harcourt Waller, Paul Leonard, and a couple of other prominent ministers, he paraded with signs at the education center, held testimonial dinners for McMillan and Bill Self, and invited Julius Chambers to become a member of his church. (Chambers declined, but enrolled his young son in the Myers Park nursery school.) Owens regarded his own gestures as feeble and symbolic. In the short run, none of them seemed to settle anything, to alter or mitigate the opposition to McMillan. In time, he hoped, the community's perceptions would change, and the judge would become an honored symbol of justice. Owens could imagine such a day, could almost feel the golden moment of triumph, but for now, in the confusion and turmoil of the early years of busing, all he could do was bear witness to the truth. So that was what he did. Other institutions, he decided, could remain silent if they chose, but Myers Park Baptist would not be among them.

Jim McMillan was grateful for that. Institutional allies were rare in those days, and indeed the only other one he could find in the months that preceded the Supreme Court's ruling was the Charlotte *Observer*. Pete McKnight was still the editor, and although he lacked the vigor of his earlier years (he was battling a disease that threatened him with blindness) he possessed a rare understanding of the sweep of Southern history. Race was the crux of it, he had always believed, and throughout his career, he had tried to address the issue forthrightly. It was a mission he shared with a few other editors—Ralph McGill in Atlanta, Harry Ashmore in Little Rock, Hodding Carter in the Mississippi delta—and together, they represented a crucial force in the South; less important, perhaps, than the beleaguered federal judges such as Jim McMillan, or the peaceful followers of Martin Luther King. But Southern editors were able, if they chose, to legitimize certain ideas for discussion—to challenge the complacency and the meanness that had paralyzed the region—and McKnight had been one of the best at that. He wrote with great realism about the Supreme Court's rulings in the fifties, and he had helped lead the fight for desegregated restaurants in the sixties. He and his executive editor Jim Batten encouraged *Observer* reporters to cover racial stories with a depth untainted by the paper's ideology. But in its opinion columns, the *Observer* was a fervent champion of racial progress, and throughout the sixties, McKnight's partner in the effort was David Gillespie, the impassioned editor of the editorial page. The two men shared the same essential values, though Gillespie brought an added indignation to the task; an outrage almost, during the busing controversy, at what he regarded as the school board's recalcitrance.

Immediately after McMillan's first ruling, Gillespie, with McKnight's strong backing, made the *Observer*'s position unmistakable: "Federal Judge James B. McMillan's opinion . . . is clear in purpose and persuasive in argument, even as it portends a difficult time for this community. There must be a new plan drawn by the Board of Education to effect faculty and student desegregation. . . . And contrary to an indication from School Board Chairman William E. Poe that the board might delay action on such a plan until public sentiment is learned, neither the board nor the school administration can waste any time before it tackles a complicated job. Poe is right in saying that difficult adjustments ordered by the court cannot be carried out harmoniously unless the public gains an understanding of the law as interpreted by Judge McMillan and cooperates in meeting the requirements of the law. But we are inclined to feel that the board's first responsibility in this instance is to lead."

When it became clear that Poe would lead in a defiant direction, resisting McMillan as much as he could, Gillespie accused him—and the school board majority—of compromising their credibility and threatening "severe damage to a sense of 'law and order' . . . the atmosphere of reason and amity in the community." On other occasions, he criticized Poe for being "petty," and the school board majority for throwing "temper tantrums."

Such opinions were bitterly resented by thousands of Charlotteans, and represented a sharp contrast with the Charlotte *News*, where editor Perry Morgan was a close friend of Bill Poe and an unrelenting critic of Jim McMillan. Gillespie, though, never doubted that he was right, and there was a part of him that relished the combat. He was a deeply ethical man, the son of a Presbyterian minister, and he had spent his boyhood in the mill town of Gastonia, where you had to be a little bit tough to survive. Pete McKnight found a great deal to admire about Gillespie, and always had. But as time went by he began to worry about the *Observer*'s editorials—not so much the substance or the thrust, but the tone that Gillespie seemed determined to adopt. "Dave has let Perry Morgan get under his skin," McKnight used to say. It was hard for him to explain exactly what he wanted, but he thought Gillespie's editorials had become too personal, too involved in the fray, when McKnight wanted the *Observer* to try to rise above it. Soon, to the dismay of colleagues who admired them both, a wintry distance grew between Gillespie and McKnight, and the tension began to mount in the *Observer*'s offices. Perhaps it was simply the nature of the times; the whole community, after all, was rife with division and turmoil. But Gillespie was still shocked one summer morning in 1971, when he came to work and found a note in his typewriter. The note had been left there by Pete McKnight, and it carried a startling piece of news: it was time to make a change, McKnight had written, and soon there would be a new editor of the editorial page. That was all. Just a note. No real expression of regret, no face-to-face explanation until Gillespie asked for one, no apparent recognition of ten years of service. Just a few awkward words on a half sheet of paper.

Gillespie was surprised and wounded. He had always known that there might be a price associated with his support of integration, but it had never occurred to him that it would take such a form. He left the *Observer* in dismay (eventually winding up at Raleigh's *News & Observer*, where he performed with distinction), and as he packed his things to leave Charlotte, he could not help but wonder what would happen next. Would McKnight back away from his support of McMillan? Would the *Observer* lapse into a silence that would betray its rich history? The answer to those questions turned out to be no. McKnight replaced Gillespie with Reese Cleghorn, an elegant and principled Southern editor from Atlanta, who possessed, as one of his colleagues would later describe it, "a quieter passion and a more measured tone." Under Cleghorn's leadership, and with the active advice and consent of McKnight, the *Observer* continued its defense of racial integration. But the coldness and the pain of Dave Gillespie's leaving was one more reminder, if another were needed, that Charlotte's ordeal could bring out the worst, could make people do things they would later regret.

Fortunately, it could also bring out the best, and even very early, that began to happen in Charlotte. There were hundreds of young parents who, if they could not yet muster full sympathy for the judge, were nevertheless determined to save the public schools. Some of them were wealthy and prominent, people who could easily have afforded the flight to private academies, and who may have even been attracted to the status of the growing number of such schools in Charlotte. Bob Culbertson, for example, was a popular Republican, a successful accountant who lived on a tree-lined street in a place called Eastover, one of the most exclusive neighborhoods in the city. He was a handsome, friendly man who had worked hard for his money and was proud of what he had been able to accomplish. As a child growing up in Albany, Georgia, he had battled with a learning disability that made reading difficult despite his I.Q., and so the trappings of wealth—the demonstrations of achievement that went along with it—meant more to him than they did to some people. For that reason among others, it was not easy for him when the schools were fully integrated in 1970, and many of his neighbors began to flee to private schools. He felt substantial peer pressure to join the exodus, for he discovered that his neighbors weren't content to leave the public schools and let it go at that. They *lobbied* those around them, incessantly and judgmentally, about the wisdom and the correctness of a private education. But Culbertson resisted the appeal, even when every child on the street except for his four had been enrolled in private schools. It was hard for him then to explain his decision, to find words for the feelings that caused him to reach it. But along with his wife, Peggy—a woman of attractiveness and a steely sense of purpose—he believed that public schools were inseparable from the promise of America. The strength of the country was its melting pot tradition—the great infusions of economic and social vitality that came with the spread of the American dream—and the rush to private schools, in Culbertson's view, represented a step toward a divided and class-conscious society.

"If you have a commitment to Americanism, and that's what I think it is," he would later explain, "then you have to ask, 'what am I willing to sacrifice for that?' And one answer is, 'the very least I can do is support the public schools.'"

So Culbertson kept his children in the public classroom, even when they were threatened or roughed-up in the early racial fighting, or later, when they were assigned to a tough junior high near a black housing project. He urged his friends and neighbors to do the same, joined a Citizens Advisory Group seeking to find a solution to the busing turmoil, and in 1974, ran successfully for the school board. The more active he became, the more he discovered that he was not alone. In 1970, during the troubled and uncertain opening weeks of school, there were four thousand volunteers, pitching in to help wherever they were needed—mothers and fathers unloading new furniture or cleaning up playgrounds, stacking new books on the library shelves. Nor did the interest peak and quickly wane. Every year the ranks of the volunteers grew larger, and many of those parents, though apprehensive initially, were not at all disappointed with what the schools had to offer.

"Public school was going to be our sacrifice," said Ward McKeithen, a white lawyer and parent, a friend of Bob Culbertson's later elected to the school board. "I don't want to sound sanctimonious about it, but my wife and I had strong feelings about the ethical issue of integration, and we thought it was imperative to support the public schools. But if that decision was our hardship, our inconvenience factor, I felt a little like we were Br'er Rabbit."

One reason that McKeithen felt that way is that his young children were assigned to Billingsville Elementary, where the principal was a black woman named Kathleen Crosby (Kat, as most people called her) who was typical of hundreds of school system professionals in her energy and dedication, and in the complexity of the problems she was called upon to solve. Billingsville was an old school, barely more than a stone's throw from Eastover, but it was across a shallow creek and a major thoroughfare, and it had long been one of the most flagrantly segregated schools in the system. Surrounded by larger and wealthier white neighborhoods, it served an island of blacks in a community called Griertown. A few well-known black professionals lived there, people such as James K. Polk, a successful businessman who was one of the original plaintiffs in the *Swann* lawsuit. But by 1970, when the first white students arrived, the income level of the neighborhood had begun to go down, and the school suddenly served an awkward mix of students: blacks from nearby who were most often poor, and whites bused from areas that were far more affluent. Still, Mrs. Crosby knew both groups brought important strengths to the school: The whites came with money and clout and high expectations for the education of their children; the blacks with a history that was long and sacrificial.

Billingsville was built in 1927, and it was a Rosenwald school, part of the philanthropic dream of Julius Rosenwald, a Jewish merchant from Springfield, Illinois, who moved to Chicago and became president of Sears and Roebuck in 1908. He was extravagant in his philanthropy and used a part of his wealth to build five thousand schools for black children in the South. Twenty-six of those schools were in Mecklenburg County, and few were the object of more pride than Billingsville. It was built on a piece of land made available by Sam Billings, a former slave who had gotten hold of some property on the outskirts of Charlotte and had farmed it profitably for much of the twentieth century. Mr. Billings was an impressive-looking man in his bibbed overalls or in a suit behind the wheel of his new Buick. Large and robust at an age when many began to falter, he raised cotton and truck crops, and lived in a big frame house flanked on a hill by two water oaks. Along with influential neighbors like Arthur Grier, who had lived in the area since 1908, he was committed to an independent future for blacks, and nothing was more important to that future than the Billingsville school.

From the time it opened, the people of Griertown had struggled to make it the best that it could be. They had raised enough money to build a brick veneer around the wooden frame, and in the fifties and sixties, after Billingsville had become a part of the public school system, people like Jim Polk, Arthur Grier's great-nephew, had pushed for such amenities as a school cafeteria.

The task for Kat Crosby in 1970 was to integrate the strengths that came from such a history with the new resources made available by the presence of whites. It was a test case, really, for the vision of Thurgood Marshall, Julius Chambers, and the other great strategists of the NAACP: the belief that it was imperative to put whites and blacks together under the same school roof, for only then would the terrible inequity of resources disappear—and perhaps also the chasm of mistrust that held the races apart. But when Mrs. Crosby first walked through the doors of Billingsville, the chasm, if anything, seemed to be growing wider.

She had arrived in mid-year—February 1971—after John Phillips and Bill Self had called her downtown and said there were some problems that they thought she could solve. It didn't take her long to see what they were. White parents were so terrified that they were actually guarding their children in the classrooms, staying with them all day to make certain they were safe. The blacks, meanwhile, simply felt invaded—their school appropriated by unwelcome outsiders—and the teachers caught in the middle were dispirited and confused. Mrs. Crosby was stunned. She had never been a principal anywhere before, much less in a situation like that. "It took me about two weeks," she says, "to decide whether to go crazy or meet the challenge."

Once the decision was made, she took the school by storm. She began a series of meetings with the relevant groups—the white parents first, telling them that they needed to be less obtrusive, more trusting of the staff, more sensitive perhaps to their black counterparts. Then the black parents, urging them to remember that it was still their school, and nobody could, or wanted, to take it away. And finally the teachers: work a little harder, she said, remember the importance of what you are doing, and hang in with blind faith if that's all you have. After all of that was done, she began a campaign to get to know the students, teasing them in the hallways, calling them "Brother" or "Sister" and telling them that Billingsville students were the best learners in the world. None of that was extraordinary, of course. It was the sort of thing any principal would do, and there were similar dramas throughout the school system. The important thing was to convey a sense of *possibility*—overpower the gloom and the pessimism with a realistic enthusiasm about how things could be. And at Billingsville, it worked. The morale of the teachers began to improve, and the antagonisms among the parents began to dissipate. The PTA was soon fully integrated, with white and black co-presidents serving side by side, and together, they tackled the problem of second-class facilities, expanding the library and the school cafeteria. And most important of all, after several years of such efforts, student test scores rose above the national norm.

Even then, however, there were still some skeptics in the community at large. At a school board meeting in 1973, a handful of parents gathered to protest the reassignment of their children. They were being moved from Eastover—the prestige public school—across the creek to Billingsville a mile or so away. It was hard to argue that the assignment was unjust, or represented a great hardship in terms of the bus ride. The families lived as close to Billingsville as they did to Eastover. But they simply didn't want to see their children moved, and as they went through their contorted rationalizations, Mrs. Crosby was watching the board meeting on her TV at home. Affronted, she got in her car and drove to the education center, where she walked boldly to the lectern and announced her disappointment: All these mamas and daddies, she said, *complaining* because their children were being sent to her school. Well, it was true enough that there was garbage in the streets—the city fathers wouldn't clean it up—but once you got inside, once you kicked away the trash and made it to the building, they had some *learning* going on. And if the Eastover parents wanted to be a part of that, if they wanted their children to share in the experience, she wanted them to know that they would be most welcome.

To some, it sounded feisty to the point of arrogance, but there was an infectious good humor in Kat Crosby's style—a contagious air of self-confidence and generosity. Through the sheer force of her personality—a competence, she says, that was patterned from her father's—she kept white flight to a minimum at Billingsville, and the school became a model of successful integration. She had a lot of help from the teachers, of course, and there were parents white and black who, as far as she could tell, simply didn't know the meaning of prejudice. For many of those involved in transforming the school, it was an experience that deeply affected their lives. Ward McKeithen said it made him feel that fundamental change was really possible in America—that the civil rights dreams of the fifties and sixties, those notions of justice on which he had come of age, were no longer a fantasy beyond the nation's grasp.

McKeithen was not alone in feeling that way, for Kat Crosby was not alone in her effectiveness as a principal. There were dozens of others with their own distinctive styles, and the accumulated effects of their leadership—overshadowed for awhile by the violence and the protests—gradually became a counterforce to the tension, adding hope to an atmosphere of gloom and resignation. And yet, the reality of resistance was present also. There were still riots in the schools, still angry rallies by the CPA, and among many parents, still a lingering distaste for the radical nature of the change. The next political test of those emotions came in the school board election of 1972. The question, as the voters prepared to cast their ballots, was which of the conflicting forces would prove to be the strongest.

Dick Spangler thought it was time for a change. The violence and turmoil of the past two years were unlike anything he had seen in Charlotte, and he had lived in the city for most of forty years. So he announced on February 2, 1972, that he was running for the school board.

Spangler had never sought or held public office, for he was a quiet man, stiff and shy when it came to public small talk, and there was nothing of the politician's flair in his bearing or appearance—in the pinstriped suits and stiffly combed brown hair which, in its styleless perfection, seemed to embody his whole personality. But Spangler did possess a powerful sense of duty, and also a willingness to make tough decisions. He had been taught at the Harvard School of Business, where he got his master's degree after graduating from the University of North Carolina, that there was never enough information on which to base a choice. But if you were going to be successful or effective, you simply had to *act*—to assess the situation with all the wile, imagination, and integrity you could muster, and then take responsibility for whatever happened. He had no way of knowing, of course, that those particular principles—and the skill and self-confidence with which he applied them—would lead him first to the vice-chairmanship of the Charlotte school board, then to the chairmanship of the state board of education, and finally, in 1986, to the presidency of the University of North Carolina. In 1972, Spangler was not especially concerned about the future—not his own, at least, for the uncertainties of the present were far too compelling.

Spangler was no particular fan of busing, though he did possess a sensitivity to the times, having been a deacon at Myers Park Baptist Church and having admired the moral vision of Carlyle Marney and his successor, Gene Owens. He disagreed with them some: They were far too interested in symbolic gestures, but they were right about moral obligations of the faith. "To whom much is given, of him will much be required." It was the gospel underpinning of noblesse oblige, and Spangler understood the concept. Both of his children were in the public schools, the schools were in trouble, and he was in a position to do something about it. That set of circumstances didn't leave him much choice.

"It's a public school world," Spangler said in his campaign, "and I want my children to learn in this world." When he spoke of such things, he had in mind something more than the melting pot theories of his friend, Bob Culbertson. Spangler believed more than most Charlotteans in the academic potential of public education. The course offerings were far broader than anything offered by even the finest private academies, and the sheer numbers of students meant that in the public school classes for the academically gifted, there would be more bright students, more inquiring minds to challenge his own children, than they would ever find in the protective confines of private education. So for all of those reasons, he offered himself as a candidate, believing that in one sense he embodied—and in another, he could shape—the white community's response to the issue thrust before it.

He talked about busing only when he had to. "The Supreme Court," he said, "has decided this matter, and we must now carry out the law. The important thing is what kind of school we have when the children get there."

Spangler was not alone in taking that approach. A young black banker named Phil Berry, an articulate housewife named Marylyn Huff, and, perhaps most importantly, School Board Chairman Bill Poe all framed the issue in precisely that way. For Poe, that was a change. He had battled the busing order all the way to the Supreme Court, but the court had now spoken and it was time to move on. The community, he said, "is telling us to stop worrying about things you can't do anything about, and get on with things you *can* do something about."

There were others who rejected that analysis: Wade Fox, Gabe Hartsell, and Gardner McCrary all had the support of the antibusing groups, and all sought to make busing a campaign theme. When the votes were counted, however, the community's verdict was clear. Bill Poe was elected outright, with Spangler, Huff, Berry, and Fox in a four-person runoff. Hartsell and McCrary were far back in the field. Then in the runoff, won by Spangler and Berry with Huff a close third, Fox and his antibusing sentiments were rejected overwhelmingly. What had happened? What sort of change had taken place in the two short years since the CPA sweep of 1970? "People have become complacent," the CPA's Don Roberson asserted. But it was obviously something more subtle than that, something far more profound. Slowly the mood of the city had begun to change, as the struggle to save the public schools—to see them through the turmoil—became a force to rival the resistance to busing. It was not, in the beginning, the *opposite* of resistance; many public school supporters did not approve of Judge McMillan's order and would have avoided the upheaval if the option had been available. But it wasn't—especially not after the Supreme Court had ruled, and the question for the community was what to do next. Was there any point in continuing the CPA resistance, or was it time now for a new kind of leader, more pragmatic and less emotional, who could try to find a solution to the school system's ordeal?

Dick Spangler saw an irony in the community's answer. By the time the CPA slate had taken office, on December 8, 1970, its most visible and newsworthy member was no longer Tom Harris, with his basic good humor and his air of moderation. Nor was it Jane Scott, for whom politeness and decorum were deeply held values. Instead, it was William Booe, who brought to Charlotte politics a kind of viciousness and hostility that were not the city's style. On the national level, perhaps, such qualities were acceptable: Jesse Helms and George Wallace were unrelentingly belligerent, and that was one thing. But Bill Booe was far closer to home, and he seemed out of control sometimes, so blinded by rage that he was oblivious to the elemental demands of diplomacy and thus was ineffective.

At his first meeting on the board, he had lashed out not only at Judge McMillan, whom nobody seemed to like, but also at Superintendent Bill Self, a popular and sympathetic figure in Charlotte. He grilled the superintendent, whom he regarded as too soft in his resistance to busing, for nearly half an hour, treating him like a hostile witness in the courtroom, until finally board member Julia Maulden felt compelled to intercede. Mrs. Maulden was a formidable person on such occasions. She was gray haired now and faintly schoolmarmish, and for the first sentence or two her voice sounded meek. But she possessed also a gentle indignation firmly rooted in principle, and even Bill Booe was impressed by her wrath. She declared on December 8 that she had been on the school board through some strife-ridden times, but never had she seen anything like this. "Mr. Booe," she said, "is accustomed to the atmosphere of the courtroom . . . and his manner of interrogation is offensive. Our superintendent is not on trial." Her sentiments were echoed the same week by Perry Morgan, the conservative editor of the Charlotte *News*, who declared editorially: "Membership on the board does not grant [Mr. Booe] license to berate, undermine and attempt to intimidate the superintendent of schools or the other members of the school staff. But that is precisely what Booe chose to do. His intensive questioning of Superintendent William Self was not the hard questioning that seeks truth. It was the loaded, leading, hostile cross-examination used in the courtroom when one wishes to destroy not only the witness's testimony, but his credibility as well. That a rookie on the board would presume to so treat a man with a long record of service is incredible."

Incredible or not, it was Bill Booe's style, and it did not change in the face of criticism. He became, if anything, even more belligerent over time, and as Dick Spangler joined the board and began to understand the effect that Booe was having, he could only smile. Tom Harris, or Jane Scott, or even Sam McNinch, with his country-boy geniality, could have been effective board members in the antibusing cause. But they were so overshadowed by Booe, whose persistent ill temper dominated the headlines, that their cause itself became lost in the furor. When you added to that the finality and unanimity of the Supreme Court's ruling, resistance came to seem both distasteful and doomed, and a mood of resignation settled over the community.

The issue, however, still refused to die. The question now—and it had become the new source of the school board's distress—was how to devise a plan for integration that would satisfy the federal courts once and for all, while at the same time winning broad community support. Eventually, the board, with the help of an unlikely alliance of citizens, did produce a plan that would accomplish all of that. But it took a full three years after the Supreme Court's ruling, and for much of that time the standoff between the board and Judge McMillan was every bit as bitter as it had been early on.

The source of the new conflict was the board's effort in the spring of 1971 to devise a different plan for desegregation. Tom Harris was heading a five-person committee assigned to that task, and along with the other members of the group, conservatives Jane Scott and Sam McNinch and liberals Carlton Watkins and Julia Maulden, Harris was drawn to Bill Self's idea of a "feeder" plan. It was a notion Self had first advanced to two of his assistants, Chris Folk and John Phillips, as they drove to a meeting in Greensboro. The idea was that students from a given elementary school, whether they lived in the immediate neighborhood of that school or not, would all be assigned to the same junior high; and students from that junior high would then be assigned to the same high school. That way, even if students were bused, they would know from the beginning which schools they would attend, and they would remain for twelve years with the same group of peers.

Jim McMillan had no problem with the concept, but when the details of the plan were presented, on June 17, 1971, the judge was astonished and outraged by what he considered an act of bad faith. The school board had rearranged assignments so that nine elementary schools in black neighborhoods would serve only grade six. Whites, as a result, would be bused into those neighborhoods for only one year, while young black students would be bused out for five. More than that, McMillan said, those whites who would be bused into black areas of town generally came from working-class neighborhoods in the northern and western parts of the city. Students in the more affluent southeast quadrant of the county (home to six of the nine board members) would rarely be bused from their neighborhoods.

Not only was the plan unfair, McMillan said, it was also inherently unstable, an invitation to a new kind of white flight *within* the school system, a chance for hundreds of white parents to move from areas where their children were bused to sanctuaries in other parts of town. "It is apparent," McMillan wrote, "that the feeder plan puts increased burdens of transportation upon black children and upon children in certain low- and middle-income white communities; that it relieves the vast majority of students of the wealthiest precincts in southeast Mecklenburg from any assignment or transportation to formerly black schools."

Over the next two years, the school board gave ground grudgingly on that point, still proposing plans that limited the busing of the most affluent students. Poe argued bitterly that McMillan was now trying to achieve "economic integration," a shift of ground that went far beyond any constitutional requirement. And Tom Harris, who thought it a considerable concession to abandon the rhetoric of his antibusing crusade and to take the lead now in devising a whole new plan to keep the buses rolling, declared with some fury that he simply didn't intend to compromise further. But the moderate voices on the board, strengthened by the arrival of Dick Spangler and Phil Berry, continued to counsel against outright defiance, and by the late spring of 1973, even the conservatives seemed anxious for a settlement. But what were the options? What would Judge McMillan accept, and would it match what the community was willing to tolerate?

"It's not our school system, Judge," Sam McNinch declared at yet another hearing on May 9. "It's not yours. It belongs to those people out there. . . . What can we do to give it back to them?"

That was the question that hung over the community, and on through the summer of 1973, the school board and the judge could not agree on an answer. There was still the mistrust, still the old tug-of-war dating back four years. But in a number of neighborhoods scattered around Charlotte, there were more and more citizens to whom the answer was obvious. And they were determined already to make their voices heard.

8

Crossing the Chasm

Maggie Ray thought the times were very strange. For the last couple of years, there had been a few defenders of Judge McMillan—Gene Owens and Pete McKnight came quickly to mind—and there had been even more defenders of the schools. Bob Culbertson and others had refused to leave them, principals and teachers had worked at building trust, and judging from the 1972 election, the community was losing a little of its anger. Yet somehow all of that didn't seem to be enough. No one so far—not Judge McMillan with his Presbyterian patience, not William E. Poe with his Baptist strength of will—had found a way to bridge the chasm, that yawning gulf of mistrust between the school board and the judge. The irony of it was that the more important chasm had already been crossed. The historic separation between blacks and whites, the pointless distance and the destructive refusal to understand their common ground, had begun to disappear; and after several years of slow, almost glacial alterations of mood, the community seemed poised on the brink of major change. What was needed now was a leader to make it happen.

It was hard to say when Maggie Ray first saw herself as that leader. The very idea made her laugh sometimes. She was a young housewife, thirty-two and pretty, with a winning smile and friendly eyes, and she did not look much older than she had in college. She had spent most of her life in Charlotte, except for her time at Agnes Scott and some travel overseas just after graduation, and she lived now in a handsome brick house with a deck on the back and a large, sloping yard overhung with oaks. Her husband Tom was a lawyer and a civic-minded man, a member of the Housing Authority and Charlotte's leading advocate of scattered public housing. Maggie shared his commitment to the city, and in her mind, there was no problem more critical than the preservation of the schools. It didn't matter that her children were too young to attend them. That wouldn't always be the case, and in any event the crisis was now.

It was not, however, a crisis beyond hope of solution, for the chemistry was already different in Charlotte. If anybody had any doubts about that, all they had to do was visit a couple of school board meetings, or read the accounts in the morning newspaper. The meetings were besieged as usual by angry white parents—large delegations from Devonshire, Hampshire Hills, and Hidden Valley, three north Charlotte neighborhoods where blacks were moving in and whites were moving out, and where the CPA had once enjoyed strong support. Yet here was Bruce Patterson, a leader from Hampshire Hills—a white ex-marine, handsome and dark haired, and obviously full of anger—telling the school board on June 12: "Judge McMillan is the last hope of sanity for our schools."

The board, he said, and not the judge, had devised the details of the current busing plan, and the board was therefore the enemy of fairness: a collection of rich white people whose motive was to protect their own parts of town. "I am not asking, and I am not pleading," Patterson said. "I am *demanding* that the board take immediate action to insure fair busing for all citizens, black and white."

Patterson's anger was reminiscent of the antibusing militants, but the substance of it was entirely the opposite. His was not a plea for the end of integration. It was a demand for simple fairness: fairness and stability, the new battle cry of blacks and whites across the city.

There was a lot of subtle history leading up to that demand, and Maggie Ray had studied it carefully. She had to. By the end of 1973, she had become the leader of a semiofficial Citizens Advisory Group, a diverse and ad hoc collection of people whose job was to advise the school board on a new plan for integration. The CAG would eventually succeed in its ambitious undertaking, devising a plan that would satisfy both the community and the judge. Mrs. Ray saw that as a staggering achievement, but the ingredients of it, she was quick to acknowledge, had taken shape much earlier.

Though no one quite realized it at the time, the momentum began to

build on May 10, 1973, when an English professor by the name of
Julian Mason—a mild-mannered man, or so he seemed—wrote a letter
to the school board. "It is time," he said, "that the primary burden of
desegregating the schools be shifted from the northern section of the
community and be more equally shared by the southern section. . . .
Feeling is high and growing."

Mason was alarmed by his community's new anger. He lived in Bruce
Patterson's neighborhood, Hampshire Hills, having moved back there
in 1970 after several years in Washington, D.C., and he had been
shocked at the time by the racial hostility. It was the first year of busing
in Charlotte, and in an atmosphere inflamed by CPA rhetoric, school
buses were sometimes surrounded and stoned, their windows shattered
by middle-class mobs. In those days, Mason felt a deep estrangement
from his neighbors. He came from a poor white family in eastern North
Carolina, but in the course of his pursuit of a Ph.D. he had become
intrigued by the literature of black America. He wrote his dissertation
on "The Critical Reception of American Negro Authors: 1800–1885,"
and later edited a volume of works by Phillis Wheatley, the African-
born poet of the eighteenth century.

During the antibusing spasms of 1970, Mason felt helpless to change
anyone's mind. He and his wife simply went about their business, doing
what they could to make integration work. Elsie Mason, who shared her
husband's white rural origins, became PTA president at Double Oaks
Elementary, a formerly black school in a declining neighborhood. She
refused to accept the job unless a black copresident was named to serve
with her, and later, when the school board debated closing Double
Oaks, the Masons became active in the effort to save it.

They were pleased when the tensions finally began to subside, but
disturbed in the spring of 1973 when there was more ugly talk around
the community swimming pool. Mason worried over the tone of the
outcry, the echoes of the racism of 1970, but this time he shared the
fundamental grievance. It seemed that every time the school board
needed white students to correct the declining ratio at a formerly black
school, they looked to the working-class areas of north and west Charlotte, and never, or almost never, did they reassign students in the more
affluent southeast.

Since the beginning of the *Swann* case, high school students in the Hampshire Hills area had been assigned to three different schools in a three-year period; and now in the spring of 1973, the school board was proposing a fourth reassignment—to West Charlotte this time, a formerly black school in a black neighborhood. Mason was infuriated by the unfairness of it, and he embarked in May on a lone-wolf crusade, first writing to the school board, then paying a visit to Judge McMillan, and finally, on May 24, showing up at a hearing in McMillan's court. During a break, he approached Julius Chambers and firmly announced, "I want to go on the stand." Chambers was puzzled. He had never seen Julian Mason before, and was unaccustomed to such offers from anonymous white people.

"Why do you want to do that?" Chambers asked.

"I'm a friendly witness," Mason replied, and on a sudden hunch, Chambers decided to take a chance.

To his pleasant surprise, Mason was effective in his testimony. He was earnest and blunt and provocative at times, the kind of witness who captured the news media attention.

"We have developed," he said, "a good situation in our area. But it has already begun to deteriorate because everyone . . . is angry. The people feel that the desegregation of schools is not being fairly shared. They feel more and more that the southeast is sheltered, and suspect more and more correlation between where the school board lives and what areas escape."

When board attorneys objected, McMillan overruled them. It was clear that the judge was intrigued by Mason's testimony, and Mason saw considerable hope in that. He began to see McMillan as an ally in the pursuit of fairness, and after the visibility of his court testimony, he discovered that he was not alone. There were others in north Charlotte who shared the same perception.

Several ministers—Presbyterians David Frye and Carl Ezzell, Methodist Tom Sigmon, and an Episcopal priest named Merrill Miller—had begun to nurture an unlikely ambition. They hoped to rechannel the anger that was sweeping through their area, building on the energy, but redefining the issue, so that the direction of protest would become less racist. David Frye soon became the most visible of the four, for he embodied most intensely the aspirations of the group. He was a smallish man with sloping shoulders and a high-pitched voice. A native of Michigan, he had spent seven years in the 1960s working in the ghettos of Terre Haute, Indiana. There, he had been shamed by the rhetoric of black power, and after he became the campus minister at the University of North Carolina at Charlotte, the same institution where Julian Mason taught English, he was obsessed for a time by the guilt of his race.

His own grandfather, a Michigan railroad worker, had been a member of the Ku Klux Klan, joining the organization in 1928, during the Depression-era migration of blacks to the north. The Klan had thrived in the competition for jobs, injecting race into an issue where it didn't belong. That, in Frye's estimation, was a depressingly common theme in American history: the failure of whites and blacks to define the right enemy, to see the common ground. It had happened in Charlotte during the first stages of busing, and now it was on the verge of happening once again.

But as Frye and the other ministers began to talk about it, and as Julian Mason and Cloyd Goodrum, a professor of mathematics, began to join their discussions, they began to consider a different possibility. Perhaps this time they could build an alliance of genuine self-interest, a coalition of blacks and whites in the less affluent parts of town. Both groups had seen their children bused away to alien neighborhoods: in the case of blacks, it frequently happened for all twelve grades, and among whites in certain areas of north and west Charlotte, children were often bused for five to eight years. For people like Julian Mason and David Frye, the issue was not busing, it was justice: the more affluent white children were seldom bused at all.

So members of the group began attending community meetings in Hampshire Hills, Devonshire, and Hidden Valley, speaking frequently and well, and lobbying their neighbors one-to-one—emphasizing the shared injustice among blacks and whites in their part of town, and emphasizing also that Judge McMillan was not the enemy that the CPA had once declared him to be, but a powerful ally of those seeking fairness.

Julian Mason was surprised at first when the message took hold, but when he thought about it, he realized that he and the others were armed with at least two things: The first was the ability to use words and numbers. They were ministers and teachers trained to think analytically, to command the statistics and the data to support their point of view. It was not necessary to their role as leaders to supply the passion or stir the troops to action; the anger and the energy were already there, and the only need at this point was to give them new shape. And the second greatest ally in that undertaking was the failure of the vision of the CPA. The great protests of three years earlier had produced nothing but turmoil, and after the Supreme Court's ruling of 1971, resistance no longer seemed to offer much hope.

There was hope, however, down the road of coalition, and it took hold quickly among the people of north Charlotte, spreading almost suddenly from the ministers and professors to the blue-collar workers who attended their meetings—to people like Bruce Patterson, the strapping ex-marine who lived next door to David Frye. The most dramatic expression of the new state of mind came at a school board meeting on Wednesday, May 30, when more than one hundred white people gathered from Devonshire and Hampshire Hills, and a few more from Hidden Valley—a neighborhood where, despite its natural integration, children were bused away for most of their schooling. There was also a smaller delegation from Druid Hills, a black neighborhood not far from Hidden Valley, and the spokesman for that group was Kathleen Crosby, the respected principal of Billingsville Elementary. Mrs. Crosby looked handsome that night. She was a tallish woman, forty-seven years old, with flashing eyes and a ready smile and high cheekbones that looked almost Indian. As she began to speak, it was clear that she was angry, and yet there was something about her style that softened the effect, a humor and geniality that seemed to make people like her, even when she was scolding. Her words tumbled out, rapid-fire and disorganized, but the room grew silent as she declared: "If you want to look for inequities, honey, you don't have to look any further than the black section of town. We are bused out of our neighborhoods for ten and sometimes twelve years. I have always urged my children to make the changes peacefully and obey the law. But I can't tell them to sit back and meekly accept all this."

When the speech was complete, there was a split second of silence, a subtle beat of hesitation, and then the hundred or so white people who had gathered from north Charlotte suddenly rose to their feet in a thunderous ovation. Mrs. Crosby was visibly astonished. "I couldn't believe it," she said the next day. "There I was making my militant speech, and all those white folks in the audience applauding like crazy. I said to myself, this can't be happening."

For an instant, David Frye was incredulous also, grateful that he didn't have to say anything, for the emotion of the moment was nearly overwhelming—a repudiation of all the years of polarization and guilt, when he had personalized the sins of his race. Here, in one of those spontaneous demonstrations, those overflows of the spirit that you simply can't contrive, whites and blacks were united in a cry for simple justice. Frye understood that it was a new and fragile union, but he allowed himself to hope, at least for the moment, and perhaps also for the first time in his life, that it was a force so powerful that it could not be resisted.

As the weeks wore on, that seemed to be the case. Even in other areas, the sheltered and more affluent parts of the city, there was a growing feeling after that that the cause was just, that the busing plan was unfair, and that it was the duty of every neighborhood to help correct the inequity. Significantly, that was a view with at least semiofficial sanction. Several months earlier, a committee of two-dozen administrators on assignment from the school board had conducted a study of unfairness and instability in the pupil assignment plan. Their conclusions had not been very different from David Frye's: "A salient factor of the plan," the educators had written in a February report, "is that black members of the community are bearing the dominant burden of assignment change and time of transportation both in hours and years. It is also true that certain areas of the white community are bearing a burden greater than others. . . . The plan calls for the extensive assignment of the *youngest* black children out of their home neighborhood for ten (in some cases, all) of their school years. . . . The plan calls for more extensive cross-busing for the north and west sides of the city than for any other area." One solution, the report suggested, was more busing of whites in the affluent southeast.

Those were the controversial conclusions at the time, not at all popular with the school board majority, and the man most responsible for that bureaucratic courage was Assistant Superintendent of Schools John Phillips, who had chaired the committee. Phillips had been in Charlotte since 1962, and he had observed the system's progress toward successful integration. Administratively, he had worked hard over the years to help manage the change, and by early 1973, he was convinced that the city had a chance to pull it off. The crucial ingredients, he thought, were already in place. The first of those was the far-sighted decision to consolidate the city and county schools in 1960. The proponents of that decision might never have envisioned the possibility of busing, might never have conceived of anything so radical, but their decision had made it much harder to escape. For even the most vehement opponents of integration, there were only four options: the public schools of Charlotte-Mecklenburg, expensive private schools, bad private schools, or the rural and small-town schools of the surrounding counties (most of which were also integrated). Though white flight was nevertheless a problem in Charlotte, consolidation kept it manageable. In addition, Phillips believed, the city had two other irreplaceable resources. The first was the Supreme Court ruling of 1971, a final and unmistakable interpretation of the law, which enabled the school board majority to tell the resisters, "We tried," but made clear the responsibilities of law-abiding citizens. And finally, said Phillips, there was the extraordinary strength of board chairman Bill Poe, whose patience seemed brittle to most of his opponents, but who held together a board that was fractious and divided, when few other people would have had the same stamina.

What was needed now, Phillips thought, was one more ingredient: a fair-minded commitment to find a stable busing plan, and he was happy to have a chance to play a role in the effort.

"John Phillips," recalls David Howe, an administrator who worked closely with him, "was a very wise, broadly intelligent man. You had to work with him in order to know it."

Howe's first encounter with the depth of Phillips's character, or at least the one he remembers most clearly, came on October 27, 1972. It was a warm Friday in mid-fall, marred by racial violence at East Mecklenburg High School: the horrifying spectacle of teenage boys—and girls also—attacking each other with cold hatred in their eyes, and the staff of the school unable to control it. That afternoon, East Mecklenburg's principal, D. K. Pittman, came to Phillips's office almost a broken man. He was tall and gaunt, and he had a heart problem, and he told Phillips bleakly that he could not go on. It was not only the violence, terrible though it was. It was also the end of a dream, a philosophy of education that had shaped his career. Pittman had been determined to make East Mecklenburg a kind of public prep school, with dazzling academic standards and most of the graduates going on to college. But that seemed impossible in the era of busing, with the school suddenly overwhelmed by a different kind of student, surly young people in a great many cases, who didn't see the value of an education at all.

Phillips listened quietly. He knew that Pittman had to go and that a new acting principal had to be at the school on Monday. He called David Howe to his office, and asked him to tell John Smith, the director of the school system's mathematics department, that he needed to see him about filling in as the new principal at East. Howe didn't linger very long in the office, but he was struck by Phillips's air of gentle strength. There was no hint of irritation or impatience, no sense of a problem that merely needed a solution. "John's agenda," says Howe, "was obviously and quite simply to prevent a loss of dignity for Mr. Pittman. He had a great deal of courage in other cases where principals had to be bolstered or removed. But the need this time was to demonstrate compassion."

Given such character, it didn't surprise Dave Howe that in the pursuit of a fairer plan for pupil assignment, Phillips would put his personal credibility on the line, that he would become one of the first men of influence in southeast Charlotte to say to his neighbors, "We have to participate more fully in the city's ordeal."

Fortunately, Phillips was far from the last to take that position. On Sunday, May 20, the same weekend as the first mass meeting in Hampshire Hills, a group of sixty parents met in Eastover, an oak-lined neighborhood in southeast Charlotte that was one of the most affluent anywhere in the city. Most of the parents were worried, and some were irate. Their children had been assigned to Piedmont Junior High, an inner-city school that was one of Charlotte's most historic. Years ago, it had been all white, and on September 4, 1957, Girvaud Roberts had broken the color barrier—the same day that her brother, Gus, had entered Central High, and Dorothy Counts had been spat upon at Harding. But the neighborhood had changed in the intervening years. A nearby housing project, Piedmont Courts, had slowly shifted from white to black, and the area around it had become riddled with crime and drugs and all the other problems of the black underclass. The school, also, had seen a decline. The red bricks were fading, graffiti marred the walls, and the halls were in need of a new coat of paint. By the time of Judge McMillan's first order, Piedmont had become a predominantly black school, and as was so often the case in Charlotte, its facilities had lapsed into inferiority. It was an unappealing place to wealthy white parents who wanted the best for their children and were accustomed to getting it. And yet the mood at the May 20 meeting was strangely accepting, strangely upbeat, despite the level of concern. Dick Spangler was there as a member of the school board and also as a resident of the Eastover neighborhood. He had voted in favor of the Piedmont reassignment, even though his own daughters, one in the third grade and the other in the sixth, stood to be affected by it within the next several years. It was their duty, Spangler thought, their opportunity to play a part in a difficult challenge, and he was not alone in that point of view. His neighbor, Bob Culbertson, spoke up as well. Culbertson was candid about his misgivings, as he and the other parents made a list of the negatives: unattractive location, inferior facilities, lack of prestige. Yet Culbertson also thought it could work. He agreed to head an eight-person committee to study the situation, and on May 24, the same day that Julian Mason testified in Judge McMillan's court about the school board's sheltering of southeast Charlotte, Culbertson and the others paid a visit to the school. They met with Piedmont's principal, Eddie Byers, along with several teachers, an assistant principal, and the leaders of the Piedmont PTA. Three days later, Culbertson offered this report: "The meeting could not have gone better. The curriculum is essentially the same as that of Alexander Graham, where our children now attend. The building looks atrocious from the outside, but it is already being renovated at a cost of about $500,000. Frankly, it looks pretty good to me, especially compared to the overcrowded A. G. The spirit seems high. . . . People seem friendlier and more relaxed. Sure, I would rather the school be in a high-income neighborhood, but I think the move can be a very good one for my children and for others."

In May and June of 1973, that spirit seemed more and more prevalent in Charlotte. "Fairness and Stability" had become a powerful new slogan—not only in the heavily bused areas of the north and west, but in the southeast as well, where many parents held their own civic-mindedness in the highest esteem, and resented the assertion that they needed to be coddled, protected from the burdens that inevitably went with change.

Still, in the minds of Bill Poe and the majority of the school board, there was reason for concern. White flight to private academies had been a problem in Charlotte, and it had occurred most seriously in the wealthy southeast. The fear of another new round, another debilitating drain of the brightest students from the system, had become an obsession for Poe and his colleagues. Even Dick Spangler still worried about it, and despite the constructive example of his Eastover neighbors, he told a reporter in June: "The razor's edge we walk is to find a way to be fair without driving more white students from the system."

Such caution infuriated the parents of north and west Charlotte, who were determined to bring increasing pressure on the board and were finding new allies all over the city. On June 12, for example, Robert Wallace, an English professor who lived in southeast Charlotte, treated the school board to a passionate lecture:

> I came to Charlotte in 1963 from the University of Alabama to take the chairmanship of the Department of English in a brightly promising new institution—the University of North Carolina at Charlotte—but also to establish my children in a humane and stable community. I knew the other kind from having been in

charge of registration at the University of Alabama when George Wallace and the national guard showed up for the governor's charade of standing in the schoolhouse door. Compared to that, Charlotte was good; but I must say to you tonight . . . that one thing has been very bad. It is the determined habit of the school board to shirk its responsibility. . . .

Allocate the burdens of busing unequally . . . and you obstinately refuse to obey the Supreme Court order. Share the burdens equally, and you comply. It is high time this board got out of the business of timid temporizing and got around to providing a stable and equitable overall plan.

Bill Poe bitterly resented such preaching. He had no use for Julian Mason, David Frye, or any of their allies. They attacked his motives and lectured him with an arrogance that was quite simply insufferable. Once, they had even bought a newspaper ad which implied a direct connection between the board members' residences (six of nine in southeast Charlotte) and the impulse to protect that part of the city. Poe responded angrily, telling a reporter who had written a story on the issue: "You write as if my entire motivation were to protect the Poe household."

If such a suggestion was a disservice to Poe, a belittling of the public spirit that burned in his heart, there was no question about the truth of a corollary point: he was deeply afraid of more white flight, and he identified with the people who were wealthy enough to flee. So he responded as he had many times in the past. Despite the logic of the coalition that opposed him, despite the eloquence of Julian Mason and Kathleen Crosby, the pressures from the judge, and the earnest conclusions of John Phillips's study, Bill Poe dug in and braced for a fight.

There was considerable history behind that decision. Poe had come to see himself as a great compromiser, a man carefully guiding the schools between the extremes. For several years now, he had lived with maddening pressures that came from two directions. From the left, there were the unrelenting demands of Julius Chambers and the stringent court rulings of Judge McMillan. Together, they had imposed radical and far-reaching changes upon the people of Charlotte, and from all indications they intended to impose even more. From the right, meanwhile, there were still the resisters. The CPA had largely disappeared, but in its place was a new organization called CUE, the Citizens United for Education, with leaders more strident than Tom Harris had ever been. At school board meetings in the early spring, spokesmen Joe Milling, Bud Johnson, and H. D. Taylor had called for an end to busing and derided the "communism" that had crept into the schools.

For Poe, after several years of such shrillness, it was all becoming just noise, and in a sense he lumped all the critics together. He understood that there were philosophical differences between Julian Mason and H. D. Taylor, but there were such similarities in their styles of attack: a rhetoric of indignation, an air of hostility toward other points of view, a tendency to belittle the motives of their opponents. And even on the board, the divisions were growing deeper. Julia Maulden, Carlton Watkins, and now Phil Berry had begun to coalesce into a committed liberal wing. Bill Booe, Jane Scott, and Sam McNinch still made up the right (though Booe often stood alone because of his abrasive personality), while Poe and a moderating Tom Harris were somewhere in between, and Dick Spangler was beginning to serve as a bridge to the liberals.

It was all very hectic and confusing, but it was the inescapable reality in 1973, as the board began to consider a delicate agenda. On April 24, Sam McNinch and Bill Booe had proposed another formal approach to Judge McMillan, an attempt to persuade him to close the Charlotte case. Specifically, McNinch and Booe were seeking an official declaration that the school system was "unitary," or fully integrated, and therefore, under the Supreme Court's 1971 ruling, was no longer required to make year-by-year adjustments—those hated annual tinkerings to preserve integration. There was an element of mischief in McNinch's proposal, for he and Booe understood that McMillan would reject it. But they saw it as the basis for a possible new appeal, and Booe defended the idea with uncommon effectiveness.

He noted that a federal judge in Greensboro, Eugene A. Gordon, had recently declared that system to be unitary, even though it operated two predominantly black schools—the same number then present in Charlotte. "Our situations are comparable," Booe asserted, "so we should decide right now to find out where we stand."

His rhetoric drew applause from the tense crowd in the room, most of them the angry white followers of H. D. Taylor. "More of the old hysteria," Dick Spangler thought sadly, as the crowd cheered Booe and hissed and shouted at everyone who disagreed. Spangler shared Booe's professed desire for a settlement of the case, but he understood also that there was a crucial difference between Charlotte and Greensboro. Judge Gordon had ruled that the Greensboro school board had "evidenced a continuing good faith implementation of constitutional principles," and thus, "the compulsion of a pending lawsuit is not necessary for this defendant to continue to act in good faith."

Good faith. Spangler knew that that was the key—a trust between the school board and the presiding federal judge—and he knew also that it simply didn't exist in Charlotte. Reluctantly, Bill Poe agreed. If the aim was really to settle the case, it was far better to delay a new appeal to McMillan, acting instead to shore up declining white ratios at West Charlotte High School and several elementary and junior high schools that fed into it. McMillan had forbidden the operation of any predominantly black schools, and if the board exhibited a good faith effort to comply with that prohibition, perhaps that would be a step in the direction of trust.

So despite the fierce pressure of more than fifty angry people, the militant CUE delegation that had filled up the board room, on April 24, Poe cast the deciding vote against the Booe-McNinch resolution. He felt a little pride at the courage that it took, and although he had no illusions about dealing with McMillan (the judge, he knew, was not an easy man to satisfy), he thought that maybe now they were on the right track.

But that was when the ground began to shift beneath his feet, as old alliances crumbled and fragile new ones emerged. The first hint that things were different came shortly after May 1, when the board voted to correct declining white ratios at four different schools. In the case of West Charlotte High, the board's method was simply to transfer black students out, not white students in. As a result, West Charlotte would have had to operate at some six hundred students below its capacity, which would have caused the loss of both teachers and courses (because, in North Carolina, teacher allocation was based on enrollment).

The West Charlotte community was outraged, and at a May 8 hearing before Judge McMillan, an honors student by the name of Kevin Barris —a white senior who ranked first in his class and who had already won a prestigious Morehead Scholarship—was called to the stand by Julius Chambers. Barris was effective, testifying quietly that because of West Charlotte's small enrollment (which would shrink still further under the school board's plan) he had had trouble scheduling the courses that he needed. That night, at a school board meeting, other West Charlotte patrons offered similar testimony, making the implicit case that since the advent of desegregation, formerly black West Charlotte had gotten worse, not better, offering fewer courses to fewer students, with fewer instructors to teach them, and all because of the school board's decisions.

For Sam McNinch that was a revelation, not at all the way things were supposed to be, and as McNinch began to talk about it, the West Charlotte crowd, which was large and mostly black, listened in amazement. Until then, they had known him primarily for his antibusing passion, and the bitter flights of rhetoric into which it could lead him. In the minds of his less sympathetic observers, Sam McNinch was stereotypical almost, with his slow Southern drawl, his seething indignation, and yet, when he felt like it, the elaborate courtliness of the old rural South. Nobody accused him of being the brightest board member, but few people who knew him seriously questioned his heart. He was a fair-minded man when he chose to be, and this, quite obviously, was one of those times.

"I should have known these things," he told the audience, "but I didn't, and it shocks me. I learned a lot in court today, and I learned a lot here tonight. I don't want you to go home without someone telling you, 'I heard you.' Well, I heard you. What you said came through loud and clear."

Bill Poe wasn't sure what to make of that. Earlier in the day, Judge McMillan was making the same points, and now here was Sam Mc-

Ninch—who had opposed everything that McMillan had ordered, everything, almost, that the judge had ever stood for—suddenly taking the same side of an issue.

Then the next day in court, things got even more strange. McNinch was called to the stand to testify, and after a few stiff and awkward responses to questions from the lawyers, he suddenly lurched free of standard courtroom etiquette.

"Your honor," he said, as he turned toward McMillan, "may I ask you a question?"

McMillan seemed surprised by the breach of protocol, but amused and impressed by McNinch's sincerity.

"Of course, Mr. McNinch," he said with a smile.

"Well," said McNinch, "after we are declared a unitary school system, does that mean we have to do nothing more?"

"A unitary system is not part of my vocabulary," the judge replied. "The Supreme Court has never said what it was without raising more questions than they answered. My approach has been to get the schools desegregated and a system designed to keep them desegregated, and then the court won't have to worry about it." McMillan added, "I am as anxious as you are to get the courts out of the education business."

McNinch expressed approval of the idea and then conceded, "I don't believe we as a school board have faced up to our responsibility to the people. It's not our school system, Judge. It's not yours. It belongs to those people out there. I would hope that you would not dictate what we do because that does not get the feelings of the people involved."

"I share that hope." McMillan responded. "And if I am satisfied that the board has taken the football and run with it, it ought to become irrelevant as soon as possible whether you have twenty-eight or fifty-four percent black in a school."

"Well," said McNinch earnestly, "I'll tell you this, Judge. There were a lot of inequities affecting black schools that I was not aware of before I came on the board. Many of them have been erased."

"An awful lot of them have been," replied McMillan. "I'm not at any time unmindful of the fact that we've come a lot further toward desegregation than any city I know of."

Still, the judge also sounded notes of caution. He said he wanted to see a full enrollment the following fall at West Charlotte High School, wanted to see southeast Charlotte more involved in the busing plan, and perhaps most importantly, wanted to see some "serious restudy" of a new plan that could "satisfy the constitutional mandate" once and for all.

When the conversation ended, McNinch was elated. He saw the day's testimony as a potential breakthrough, a major step toward trust between the school board and the judge. Bill Poe, however, remained deeply skeptical. He couldn't really see that anything had been accomplished. Judge McMillan had always been affable enough, charming and beguiling on the bench or in private. But it seemed to Poe that after every board concession, McMillan wanted more, that he always maneuvered so the board would give ground—and how was this conversation any different? What the man now seemed to be demanding, after all the board's efforts over the previous three years, was *economic* integration, and that was something Poe was not about to offer.

He would support an increase in the West Charlotte enrollment, would even send Eastover students to Piedmont Junior High, since the school was not far from where the students lived. But the new whites at West Charlotte would come from Hampshire Hills and Devonshire; they would not be bused across town from the south. In Poe's mind, he was trying to be reasonable, trying to give McMillan some of what he wanted without issuing an invitation to a new round of white flight. But as soon as the school board majority adopted that approach, they were suddenly besieged by a new set of critics, the Julian Masons and David Fryes from the middle class of north Charlotte, who were as righteous and unrelenting as any critics in the past, and who seemed to have marshaled a bewildering array of allies: McMillan, Julius Chambers, a few black leaders like Kathleen Crosby, and more tentatively perhaps, Sam McNinch and his friend Jane Scott, two of the school board's most conservative members.

By early June, Poe was angry and impatient, if not a little bit confused by the strange new refrain from Sam McNinch and others that this was "a golden opportunity" to work toward a settlement. McNinch, it seemed, had been busily engaged in a kind of maverick diplomacy, first eating lunch with McMillan after their conversation in court, and then suggesting at a school board meeting in June that four board members meet informally with the judge, and that the meeting be set for the next afternoon.

"Many of you know," McNinch told the usual overflow crowd at the school board meeting, "that I did have a discussion with the judge at a recent hearing, and I did have lunch with him several days after that. I learned a lot. I don't know how much he learned, and I say that in all sincerity, but I have to put my trust in the judge at this point."

The crowd cheered and Bill Poe grimaced. The whole idea of a chummy little meeting with the judge offended his notion of orderly jurisprudence, and more viscerally perhaps, he simply didn't feel very friendly toward McMillan—did not trust that impulse in the other board members. He called the proposed meeting a "foolish" idea, and said, "I urge the board to defeat this motion."

The board rebuffed him, however, and the next day, June 14, at 4:30 P.M., McNinch and Jane Scott, Carlton Watkins, and Phil Berry all arrived at the judge's chambers. There was a certain stirring elegance about the setting: the walnut furniture, the law books on the shelves, and just outside, the American flag and the high wooden benches of McMillan's courtroom, magisterial in their embodiment of the law. McMillan himself fit well in that environment. He possessed an air of command that he didn't have to flaunt, and though he spoke softly—so softly sometimes that you had to listen carefully to understand what he said—his words carried the force of intelligence and certainty. He was cordial this day, but unyielding as well, clear in the expectations he had already voiced: "I don't really know what I can say that I haven't already said. At the last hearing, I said that West Charlotte should be dealt with for this year by assigning white children from areas of the county where there are the fewest black children. . . . The biggest single step that can be made for the fall would be to put people into busing situations from places where they don't now have to get on the bus."

To McMillan's surprise, every board member in the room accepted that view. "My position is this," declared Jane Scott, who lived on Charlotte's West Side and resented the way her area had been treated. "Why not try, since we never have, involving some of these areas that are not bused and see how it works?" Sam McNinch agreed. He said he did not care where the board found West Charlotte's white students, "as long as they come from the closest possible areas."

"Then," said McMillan, "they should come from here." And he pointed on a map to the vicinity of Myers Park, one of the oldest and wealthiest areas of the city, not far from the heart of downtown, and, as everyone knew, home to Bill Poe. Even then, there was no dissent, and it was suddenly clear that the judge and the board were only inches apart if they differed at all. It was true that McNinch and Jane Scott were still opposed to any busing. But if the schools had to have it—and the federal courts all agreed that they did—then the board should devise a fair and stable plan. Watkins and Berry wholeheartedly agreed, and so did their friend, Julia Maulden, one of the board's staunchest advocates of desegregation. It was hard to believe, after all the years of dissension, and all the hours spent wrangling in McMillan's courtroom, that they were now on the verge of settling the case. There were more hurdles to cross, more specifics on which to agree. But under the prodding of McMillan and of citizens around the county, five members of the board —a majority—were prepared to recast the busing plan to make it more just.

Indeed, during the two-hour course of the June 14 meeting, there had been only one apparent disagreement, and it concerned an issue that was complex and arcane. McMillan had suggested that students who were bused to West Charlotte ought to be chosen in some random manner— by a lottery perhaps—from several different districts, instead of from a single district that whites could easily flee. The school board members were skeptical of that. They said they feared such a system would separate friends and add too much trauma to the transfer process.

It was nearly inconceivable that such a minor point would prove insurmountable, but that summer it did. Within a week the fragile new consensus—the painful, tentative, statesmanlike effort to cross the chasm of mistrust between board and the judge—was suddenly in ruins. And for those who viewed that development with sadness, it was hard to escape a disappointing conclusion: if it had not been for the least attractive tendencies of McMillan and Bill Poe, their translation of principle into a stubborn test of will, their personalization of a dispute to a degree that wasn't healthy, the case might well have been settled that summer.

Instead, however, the undoing of an agreement began the next morning, June 15, when Poe told a reporter: "The judge is making new law if he hands down the kind of ruling he is talking about. The Supreme Court has not talked about socio-economic integration. It's just the judge's idea of how society ought to be." Asked if he would favor appealing such an order, Poe replied without qualification: "I certainly would."

There was serious doubt, of course, that Poe had the votes to back his declaration. Five members of the board had rebuffed him once and seemed to be prepared to do so again. But Judge McMillan—infuriated by Poe's continuing opposition—did not wait to find out. On Tuesday, June 19, the day before the full board was to meet, he issued a stringent new opinion that left McNinch and Jane Scott feeling bewildered and betrayed. He ordered busing from out of the southeast. That alone was no problem. But he ordered the students chosen randomly from six different districts—the kind of lottery approach that the board members had said they could not support—and the consensus gave way to wounded confusion.

On July 2, the board voted to appeal, with McNinch and Mrs. Scott joining Poe, Booe, and Harris in a five-person majority. The five skeptics of busing were suddenly reunited; the issue was mired more deeply in the courts, and the city's mood descended to despair.

Maggie Ray shared the dark feelings of the moment, and though she was not yet involved in the case, she remembers musing about the need to find a mediator.

She had no way of knowing that she would be the one.

9

The Moment of Triumph

Maggie Ray got her chance in November. It was an accident, really, the product of the prodding of her friend Eleanor Brawley, who had come to Charlotte a year or so before, moving down from Richmond, where the public schools were in trouble. She had been told that Charlotte was more of the same, for she traveled in circles where white flight was common. Her husband Bob was a doctor, quite able to afford private schools, and for a while the Brawleys selected that option. But Eleanor was also committed to civic involvement, and she found herself drawn to the Charlotte ordeal, the city's struggle to integrate its schools.

At her church, Sardis Presbyterian, she organized some Sunday school discussions of desegregation, and along with a banker friend by the name of Gene Cathey, became involved in the school board election of 1972. Cathey had two children in the public schools, and he was convinced—and helped convince Mrs. Brawley—that white flight was a problem that required a solution. It seemed certain to grow worse in a climate of resistance, inflamed by the rhetoric of the CPA. So Cathey, Mrs. Brawley, and their friends in the neighborhood—an area deep in the heart of southeast Charlotte—put together the Committee for a Positive School Board. It was a solid, hardworking group of several dozen citizens who backed a slate of winning candidates in the 1972 election: Poe, Spangler, and young Phil Berry.

When the election was over, Cathey and Mrs. Brawley felt the need to do more, and with the help of Don Bryant, a Chamber of Commerce leader, they formed the Quality Education Committee, an ad hoc citizens' support group for schools. For several years until then, Chamber people had been largely silent on the struggles over busing, conspicuously so by the high standards set in 1963, when Pete McKnight and the business leadership joined Mayor Stan Brookshire in confronting the issue of segregated restaurants. But Don Bryant, among others, was not comfortable with the silence of the 1970s. He was no fan of Judge McMillan's orders, but national Chamber of Commerce studies had shown a clear correlation between the economic health of any given community and the support and strength of its public schools. So with the backing of Bryant and staff help from the Chamber, the Quality Education Committee began to push the cause of public education, calling attention to the need for citizen support, urging an end to the obsession with busing. Maggie Ray was a member of that committee. Its work seemed safe and at least semirelevant, and it was a comfortable way to show concern for the schools.

Then in mid-fall of 1973, things began to move rapidly. To no one's surprise, the school board lost its appeal of McMillan's June ruling, and thus the order was once again in effect. It called for major changes. In addition to the lottery assignments to West Charlotte High School, which the board had already implemented while the appeal was being heard, McMillan had required something even more drastic: a totally new desegregation plan, fairer and more stable, to be implemented in the fall of 1974. McMillan wanted to see citizen involvement in the formulation of such a plan—a desire that was partly pragmatic, partly a matter of principle—for despite widespread perceptions to the contrary, the judge was determined, if possible, to avoid the role of czar. Within the constitutional framework as he understood it, he wanted the community to find a way to settle the issue. He thought, in fact, the community might have moved ahead of its leaders: "There is an unconscious assumption on the part of a lot of people on the school board that folks with spreading lawns and big houses are more intolerant," he had told the board delegation on June 14. "I don't think that's true."

Gene Cathey and Eleanor Brawley were inclined to agree. They both lived in southeast Charlotte and both had been impressed by the openness of their neighbors, that sense of civic duty and enlightened self-interest that seemed more and more to be rising toward the surface. At a Quality Education Committee meeting in the fall, a breakfast gathering at a downtown restaurant, they agreed that devising a new plan represented an opportunity at least as much as a hurdle. Mrs. Brawley remembers telling the others in the room, "It's critical to have the community buy into the plan." She suggested that they form a Citizens Advisory Group to observe the school board's progress. Then, in a moment of sudden inspiration, her mind flashed back to an evening at Maggie Ray's—a hot dog dinner with maybe fifty other people, one of whom had been Judge McMillan. Mrs. Brawley had never seen the judge before, and he was not at all what she had expected. He was so small, for one thing, not much more than five-feet-seven, and his bearing was shy—not uncomfortable, for there was a twinkle in his eye. But all in all, there was a curious incongruity between McMillan's humility, his unassuming presence, and the vastness of his impact on the city where he lived. The thing Mrs. Brawley remembered most clearly, however, was McMillan's obvious affection for his hostess, Maggie Ray. She would have been tempted to call it flirtatious if the judge hadn't been so courtly about it, so avuncular and sweet, and so obviously devoted to his own wife Marjie. But there was no way to mistake the depth of his esteem, for the simple truth was, he regarded Maggie Ray as one of his finest young friends.

Remembering that, Eleanor Brawley nominated Maggie to head the CAG. Eleanor knew that Maggie would have the backing of the judge, and knew also that she possessed a serenity and toughness that would surely help her lead. So Mrs. Brawley and Gene Cathey took her to lunch at the Athletic Club, and they outlined the role that they wanted her to play. Maggie protested just a little, but by the time the lunch was over, she was excited by the prospect of what lay ahead. She enlisted the help of her friend Betsy Bennett, an energetic Alabamian of about the same age, and together they sent out invitations to a meeting. The notices were folksy to the point of being corny—little smiling faces and promises of a meal: "Pot luck," it said, for in Maggie Ray's experience, Southerners were always more civil over dinner.

More than two dozen people responded to the notice, and they had no way of knowing what they were setting in motion.

The meeting had been set for November 12, 1973, and the crowd began arriving at 6:00 P.M., assembling in the large and antiseptic room where the school board met at least once a week, sometimes more during times of greatest crisis, for the room was no stranger to the passions of the day. But Maggie Ray and Betsy Bennett had had enough of all that. They had grown weary of the venom of the antibusing crowds, the histrionics of Bill Booe, the brittle impatience of chairman Bill Poe. They thought the time had come to settle the issue, and they knew that these leaders had the power to do it.

The school board had invited representatives from school committees, civic organizations, the NAACP, antibusing groups like CUE and the CPA—anybody they could think of with an interest in education—to testify at a board meeting on November 20. The board members wanted, they said, citizen input on a new plan for integration, and it was the ambition of Maggie Ray, Betsy Bennett, and their friend Eleanor Brawley to forge a clear consensus in advance. Maggie thought they had a chance to pull it off. She shared the increasingly widespread notion that the community had changed—that the deep divisions of the past had finally begun to heal, or at least that the wounds were no longer as raw. And yet it was all so delicate. The crowd that had gathered on November 12, or that would speak to the board on November 20, would include H. D. Taylor, whose followers still saw busing as a communist plot. And it would include Kelly Alexander, the old warhorse from the NAACP—gray haired now, but still ramrod straight, still as passionate as he had been in 1957 when he had appeared before a different but equally troubled school board, reminding them of a ruling by a different Supreme Court, asserting the moral and legal imperative of racial integration. So much had happened since those early days. They had reached the point where the integrationists' dream was finally being tested, and Maggie thought the triumph could well be at hand. And yet it was also possible that it would all blow up—that once you assembled such a splendid microcosm of the community as a whole, and once these people began to speak out, began seriously giving voice to the things they really felt, the old fears would resurface, and all the old hostilities would suddenly reignite.

But Maggie thought she knew how to keep that from happening. She wanted to appeal to something as old and time-honored—as powerfully Southern, in its own peculiar way—as the legacy of segregation against which they were struggling. She wanted to appeal to the notion of good manners.

Maggie understood the profundity of the concept, for she was the daughter of Mr. and Mrs. Beaumert Whitton, two aristocratic Southerners who taught her by example that gentility was not a sham, that it was unseemly for self-assurance to devolve into arrogance, and that civility was the glue that held the world together. People could disagree; that was fine. They could even feel strongly about the things that they believed, and they could express those views with candor and force. At the same time, however, there was simply no denying the value of tact, and those were the lessons she intended to apply.

She decided the first step was primarily to listen, but to do it in a way that encouraged agreement. So as the crowd began to gather on November 12, moving toward the tables decorated with geraniums, each person was handed a mimeographed sheet with "INSTANT CONSENSUS FORM" typed across the top. Below were three questions: What are the worst features of the pupil assignment plan? What are the best? Do you consider yourself conservative, moderate, or liberal on school-related issues?

Maggie Ray and Betsy Bennett tabulated the results quickly, while the others were still eating their meals, and they were elated at what they found. It simply could not have gone any better. On almost every sheet, regardless of the politics of the person responding, there was agreement on the flaws of Charlotte's busing plan: too many children were taken from their neighborhoods, the bus rides were often long, and the plan was not fair—particularly to blacks, but also to whites in the northern and western parts of the city. There was agreement, also, on the things that were good: the terrible inequities that had afflicted black schools—the rubble-strewn playgrounds and the hand-me-down books, even the inferiority of some of the physical plants—had begun to disappear. Blacks and whites had gotten to know each other, and racial stereotypes had begun to break down.

"Guess what," said Maggie, in announcing the results, "we all agree."

But it wasn't just the consensus on those generalizations. During the discussion that night, and at another meeting that followed on November 19, and at the meeting with the school board on November 20, they began to notice a powerful and heartwarming chemistry, a personal affinity for each other that was sweeping through the group. Bill Smith felt it—and if you had told him beforehand that he would develop a deep personal fondness for Jim Postell, he would have said you were crazy. Smith was black, a quiet young salesman for Aetna Insurance, who lived in Hidden Valley, a changing neighborhood on the northern rim of the city. Postell was almost a neighbor. A steel company executive, he lived nearby, in a semirural area known as Hickory Grove. But he was white and full of bluster, and his political views, at least in the presence of those who agreed, were far to the right. He didn't like busing, didn't especially approve of racial integration, didn't like having a woman as the leader of their group. But there was something *real* about Postell's toughness, a substance beneath the bluster that allowed him to listen. And so it wasn't long, he later recalled, before he was "chopped plumb down on a few of my notions."

When busing first began, Postell said, he "didn't give a damn whether the schools stayed open or closed." But now, he continued, it was clear that "we'll have a better society if we assure everyone an equal education—and the federal courts aren't going to turn us loose until we show them we're really trying to do that. This is the cross of the day," he added, with a depth of sentiment that the others found affecting, "that black and white people have got to learn to live together. But it's a hard thing. Black and white is hard."

So Postell was one who wanted to keep going, wanted to formalize the group to come up with a plan, or at least a set of guidelines, that could end the busing controversy once and for all. There were others who agreed: Bob Culbertson was one, and Wilson Bryan, a conservative white Republican from northwest Charlotte; and Pat Arnold, a liberal leader in the League of Women Voters and a former school board member from White Plains, New York; and Phyllis Lynch, an articulate black militant, young and overbearing; and Mabel Dail, a middle-aged secretary, hardworking and quiet. The list went on. There were twenty-five in all, and they wanted to pursue official status as advisors to the board.

In response, Maggie Ray agreed to approach Bill Poe, whose law offices were not far from her husband's, and tell him what the group had in mind. Poe replied graciously that their idea was fine: the board, he said, could certainly use the help. Maggie thanked him and left, and soon she and her committee of twenty-five—who now called themselves the Citizens Advisory Group—were meeting once a week at the education center, gathering in a third-floor room with a table in the middle and gray filing cabinets on every side. They knew they had at least one major advantage over Poe and his colleagues: they were free from the glare of daily publicity, the houndings of the press, the anger of the crowds that still came to board meetings. They could disagree pointedly without playing for applause, without their conversations becoming contests to be won or lost. And perhaps even more importantly as time went by, they were united by the urgency of their new sense of mission. "Every single person," Maggie says today, "thought it was the most important thing that they had ever done."

The discussions, she admits, grew heated at times, but it was passion tempered by a reliable sense of humor. Postell, especially, played his role to perfection. When the rhetoric grew shrill, or the disagreements petty, he would lean back in his chair—always the same one, a secretary's chair with a deep swivel seat—and he would say in a voice filled with mock derision, "Picky, picky, picky."

That was how it went: a group of average people, not immune to prejudice, not yet free from stereotypes or fear or from the limits of vision that were the South's racial legacy; but struggling nevertheless with the most critical problem of their city. And they were making progress.

As the weeks went by, they hammered out a set of principles on which they all agreed, and one day early in 1974, Maggie met secretly with Judge McMillan. Over lunch she told him that they would urge the school board to recast its plan for desegregation, distributing the burdens of busing as equally as possible, allowing walk-in schools in integrated neighborhoods, building new schools with integration in mind, and keeping each school twenty-five to forty percent black by refusing, if necessary, any student transfers that threatened the delicate balance of desegregation. McMillan was delighted. He had already had great confidence in Maggie, and he told her that if those principles could form the basis of a plan, the end of the drama might really be in sight.

The next step, then, was to transform the principles into a concrete proposal—or at least to consider how that could be done—and for a while, the CAG had some expert help. It came from John Smith, a mathematician on the schools' central staff. He was a quiet, somewhat colorless man, with graying hair and thick glasses, every inch a bureaucrat. But he was also smart, and he had proven his mettle in the realm of integration. One October Friday in 1972, he had been called to the office of his boss, John Phillips, and he had been told that as of the next Monday, he would be the acting principal at East Mecklenburg High. The school had been closed because of racial fighting, and the principal had resigned, and it was up to John Smith to straighten things out.

When Monday came, he drove early to the school, leaving his house before the sun was up, and as soon as he parked his car—it was then nearly seven—a group of student leaders met him at the door. There were blacks and whites, and they asked his permission to put up some posters, urging a renewed dedication to harmony among the races. As Smith began talking to the students, it struck him that they had come face to face with the bitter fruits of prejudice, that they had seen how nasty the climate could become, and were determined as a result to do something about it. Over the next several months, Smith had encountered that resolution again and again among the teenagers at East. He came away from the experience with a deepened conviction that integration could work. But the success would not happen on its own, Smith thought. It would require the same effort, the same kind of wisdom, the same resolution, among the city's adults.

Unfortunately, for a while that spirit had seemed rare, but Smith thought he sensed it in the CAG. He liked Maggie Ray, and he was impressed by the seriousness of most of the others—Betsy Bennett, Wilson Bryan, and especially Bill Smith, the black insurance man. So he offered the group the full store of his knowledge, including an idea he had been working on for some weeks: a "proximity plan" for pupil assignment, a detailed, computerized study of where the students lived in the Charlotte-Mecklenburg system, and, using that data, of which assignments would most efficiently integrate the schools. The plan had some rough spots. But Smith was determined to adjust it to reality, and the CAG members were intrigued by his efforts, convinced they held the promise of a more equitable plan.

In February, however, the school board moved in another direction. On February 11, the board heard a report from the CAG, an explanation of the group's general thinking, and responded with nothing but a polite thank-you. And then on February 27, the board approved a new assignment proposal for the fall that was little more than a patchwork alteration of its old feeder plan, including, incredibly, precisely those assignments to West Charlotte High School that Judge McMillan had rejected the previous summer.

John Smith was a trooper, and accepted the board's decision with quiet good grace, but Maggie Ray was enraged. She felt that her committee had been slighted, that its counsel had been nothing more than a public relations ploy. But even more than that, she shared a kind of groaning dismay at the school board's intransigence, an astonishment that school officials would come back to McMillan with a set of assignments he had forcefully ruled out. Already, the appeals court had sustained that ruling. What in the world, Maggie wondered, could the board be thinking?

She was determined now that the CAG would move beyond the general principles it had already adopted and draw up its own specific plan, a counterproposal to the board's pathetic effort. She understood the obstacles, and the need for tact, for despite the unity they had forged within the CAG, there was still the possibility the consensus would dissolve. Once, for example, when they were wrestling with the problem of which students should go to West Charlotte, and Maggie had seemed uncertain about it, Jim Postell had grown angry and exploded: "Your neighborhood needs to go, Maggie!"

Maggie was not fazed by that kind of challenge. She knew that occasional outbursts were only to be expected, and besides, she had heard the same argument many times before, and found it persuasive. For the better part of a year—ever since those eloquent protests from David Frye and Julian Mason castigating the school board for protecting wealthy neighborhoods—she had winced at the notion of seeking special favors. Her view of privilege was very different from that, for she had absorbed a fundamental lesson from her parents: that prominence was best protected by a sense of civic duty.

So the main threat to the mission of the CAG did not come from within. Its members, quite obviously, were capable of dealing with passing moments of rancor, and there was no one in the group with a hidden agenda. The question that troubled Maggie was one of expertise—the necessity of mastering the numbers and demographics, for those things were crucial to drawing up a plan. It would have been no problem if John Smith were still around, but the word had come down that it was time to back away. "Members of the board," Smith remembers, "and some of our staff, were apprehensive. The CAG was one of these groups that wanted to *do* something, and there were those who didn't trust their experience and know-how."

As a result, Maggie and the others had to forge ahead on their own. They worked quietly and privately—still in the crowded third-floor room near John Smith's office—and even though the work was frustrating and difficult, they were making a little progress during the month of March, when suddenly and accidentally, there came a breakthrough. On March 21, Jim Postell was talking with Kathy Moore, the aggressive education reporter for Charlotte's CBS affiliate, WBTV, and he let slip the fact that the CAG was at work on a plan—that its members had felt cheated and ignored by the board of education, and intended now to do something about it. Maggie did her best to get the story suppressed. Their efforts were still in the embryonic stages, and she wanted to avoid, at least in public, an adversarial stance between her group and the board. But the story ran on the eleven o'clock news, and the papers picked it up over the next couple of days, and one of the most interested readers was Judge McMillan. His patience with the board was stretched to its limit, and now more than ever, he saw the CAG as a way to break the impasse.

He immediately began work on a new court order, and he was preparing the final draft during the first week of April, when Maggie Ray happened to appear at his office. She had come to see a map entered earlier as evidence (it was easier to see it there, she figured, than to deal with the school system's reluctant bureaucracy). McMillan smiled when he saw her, and called her into his office, and much to her surprise, allowed her to listen as he dictated his opinion.

Maggie was surprised and then elated at what the order said. The defendants, declared the judge, his voice matter-of-fact, almost a monotone, as he read the ruling aloud, "have again defaulted in an obligation to the community and to the school patrons. . . . With the board thus dedicated it would be an idle exercise to direct defendants to require their staff, unaided, to produce effective plans to eliminate the discrimination which remains or to address themselves to the unfairness which, on the presently incomplete record, appears manifest in many phases of the proposed pupil assignment plan." Therefore, the judge said, he was asking the CAG to help devise a better plan, and was ordering the school system to cooperate fully in that undertaking. Maggie smiled with satisfaction. At last, she thought, they had a little power.

Two weeks later, her husband Tom picked up the phone and called an old friend. The voice on the other end was gravelly and hard. It belonged to W. T. Harris, chairman of the Mecklenburg Board of County Commissioners, a man respected, almost revered, in Charlotte for his soaring public spirit and his hardheaded street savvy in the world of politics. "Boss," said Tom, "I need your help." And he quickly summarized the recent events in Maggie's life—the long days and nights at the Education Center, the feverish preparation of a new plan for integration. Within a few days, Maggie would have to present this proposal at a formal hearing in Judge McMillan's court. She would be subjected, Tom said, to the rigorous cross-examinations of the school board's attorneys, and while William Sturges, who had taken over the board's legal work from William Waggoner and Ben Horack, was not a vicious man, still Tom did not want Maggie on a limb by herself. He asked that Harris—"Mr. Bill," as some people called him—spend a little time around the courthouse, and help make it clear that Maggie had some friends.

Harris agreed without hesitation. Tom Ray had managed his most recent campaign, and he had always had great affection for Maggie. Besides, he said, the damn school case had dragged on long enough. It was sapping vital energy, keeping things in an uproar, when the time had clearly come for the community to move ahead. And while Harris didn't say it, he also believed that when push came to shove, it would take more than Maggie Ray to cause that to happen. Her work was important, no doubt about it. She and her colleagues had made a powerful case for fairness and stability. But the need at this point was for someone to manipulate the levers of power, and that, quite frankly, would mean someone like himself. And W. T. Harris had done it before.

He was a veteran politician, a powerful-looking man, even though at sixty-five he had a little age on him now. There was a slight stoop to his walk, and his hair was gray and thin, and there were deep vertical lines on his suntanned face. Still, there was an obvious vigor about him. His voice was strong and rich, with accents acquired during his youth in south Georgia, and there was wisdom and candor in most of what he said. He had made a lot of money in the supermarket business, but his avocation was his love of politics: not so much the matter of getting himself elected, but the opportunities that followed for getting things done.

Less than two years earlier, he had stumped the state with Dick Spangler, rallying support for the cause of public kindergartens, persuading the legislature to appropriate $12.3 million to make them a reality. "We were real proud of the General Assembly," he had declared with conviction when the effort finally ended. For that was his way: W. T. Harris was a generous man, whose need was not for public credit or acclaim; it was to indulge his affinity for doing good in the back corridors of power.

So on April 23, 1974, he made his way early to Judge McMillan's court. It was the fifth day of hearings on the new pupil assignment plan for the fall, and for the first time Maggie Ray was scheduled to testify. The hearings, until then, had been almost unbelievably tedious, with board attorney William Sturges leading a cantankerous administrator by the name of Wayne Church—a man legendary for his inability to speak a comprehensible sentence—through the intricate minutiae of the school board's plan. Judge McMillan was plainly annoyed, and it was clear to W. T. Harris that he was pleased and relieved to have Maggie on the stand. And of course, thought Harris, she was performing quite well. However terrified she may have been in advance, she was cool and composed, defending the CAG proposals with effectiveness and certainty, despite the relentless cross-examinations of the school board's lawyer.

And the proposal, in fact, did have some flaws. It was still a draft, for one thing, with no definite answers on several major points, including the crucial question of which students would be assigned to West Charlotte High School. But it also contained some promising elements: an assurance that no child would escape busing altogether, but that every child, even the blacks who had borne the biggest burdens, would attend a neighborhood school for at least three years. These features clearly fascinated the judge, and he told the members of the CAG: "To make a gross understatement about the job that you have done, I'm amazed at your thoroughness, intelligence and motivation. You may not have all the answers, but you certainly have recognized the problems and approached them frankly." He scheduled another hearing in May to allow Maggie and the others to flesh out their proposals.

Later, when the hearing had recessed that Tuesday afternoon and the reporters and photographers swarmed toward Maggie, W. T. Harris stepped to her side and draped his arm around her shoulder. He didn't say much, but the symbolism was clear—and though it may have offended some young women in that era when feminism was sharply on the rise, Maggie Ray understood it and couldn't suppress a smile of satisfaction and gratitude; for here, in his fatherly, Old South way, the most influential man in local government was sending a signal to the school board and whoever else was watching that he and Maggie Ray were on the same side.

Harris didn't stop with an act of body language. The next day, he had lunch with McMillan in the judge's chambers, and the two of them talked for well over an hour—long enough to delay the afternoon's testimony. Harris said he was tired of the way things had been going, and he knew the judge didn't want to run the schools. The time had come for "peace in the valley," so what could they do to bring it about?

The judge replied frankly, framing the issue in simple layman's terms, and Harris liked that about him. The judge was a man, and you could deal with him that way: straight-up, man-to-man, without a lot of silly games. McMillan had the cards, and he knew it. The Supreme Court had been clear, and so had his own orders, and the only obstacle to a settlement was the attitude of the board. Bill Poe was determined, if it killed him, to protect southeast Charlotte, including his own affluent neighborhood, and the simple truth was that that wouldn't do. Basic fairness demanded otherwise.

Harris got the message, and he decided it was time to present it to Poe. He knew the presentation would carry some force, for he headed the board of county commissioners, and the commissioners determined the size of the school system's budget. But that was not the point. That was not the thing that made him optimistic. Harris simply admired Poe's strength and public spirit, and he had come to know over the years that the high regard was mutual. So there would be no pulling of rank, no implied threats or intimations of pressure when the two of them met. They would sit down over lunch, one man to another, and they would try to talk it through until they finally got it straight.

Neither remembers where the meeting occurred, or precisely when, or even how many conversations there were, but both are clear on the tone and general substance. Harris was forthright about his own basic feelings. Like Poe, he was an advocate of the neighborhood school, and didn't think busing was the right thing to do. But that no longer mattered, he said. The courts had spoken. Indeed, the highest court in the land had affirmed Judge McMillan, and the question now was whether they were a lawless people in Charlotte, or whether they were not. "We've got to stand where the law is," Harris liked to say, "not just where we would like it to be."

But Bill Poe didn't need any sermons on the law. His reverence for it was the match of any man's, and that was just the point. Jim McMillan was forever overstepping himself, forever plowing new and dubious ground in his constitutional interpretations, and as a result the public schools were being badly damaged. Already, they had lost thousands of white students and they stood to lose a great many more, if the judge got his way and forced them to bus white children out of southeast Charlotte.

That was the point at which Harris got mad. He didn't raise his voice, nor did Poe in response, for their respect for each other was simply too great. But Harris had come to share Maggie Ray's understanding of fairness—her offense at preserving the sanctuaries for Charlotte's most privileged—and all of that was now entwined with his Christian understandings. He was a Baptist, like Poe, and they had taught him back in Sunday school in Cordele, Georgia, that love was the essence of what they believed. How can you say you love me, whom you have not seen, and yet you don't love your neighbor whom you have seen? And how could they read that verse in twentieth-century America and still find excuses to deny a little child? How could they call themselves Christian and free when they were still all tangled up in the issue of race? There wasn't but one way to escape that tangle, and that was for everyone to do his part, everyone to bear his fair share of the burden—and that, sad to say, was what Poe was resisting.

"Bill," said Harris, now staring at him hard, "how in the world do you justify this? I'm a Christian. I couldn't sleep at night."

It's hard to assess the immediate effect of the sermon. May and June were difficult months for Bill Poe, a time of stubbornness and a time of strength, and in that order.

On May 20, Maggie Ray returned to federal court and offered a fleshed-out version of her plan. Sure enough, it included the busing of teenagers from southeast Charlotte—from Poe's own neighborhood, in fact—to West Charlotte High School. The next day, Poe blasted the plan as "potentially a disaster," and predicted it would lead to a new round of white flight. That same week, an unpleasant assignment came down to a school administrator by the name of Ed Sanders, the same Ed Sanders who had been principal of Central High School in 1957 and who had stared into the faces of an angry white mob, laying his own safety on the line to protect young Gus Roberts. Although he had been one of the heroes in the opening round of integration, Sanders was now cast temporarily in the role of resister. By 1974, he had risen through the ranks of the Charlotte-Mecklenburg system, performing a variety of administrative duties, and now as associate superintendent of schools, he had been ordered to lead the official assault against the CAG, to pick out the weaknesses in the advisory group's plan. At a school board meeting on May 28, Sanders echoed and expanded Poe's objections. He conceded the CAG plan was fair, but argued at some length that it was unstable and unworkable. "In our opinion," he said, "the price for it would be very great."

By the end of the week, however, Sanders had had a change of heart. He had become convinced, and had firmly told Poe, that the board and CAG could work out a compromise. The pivotal moment in Sanders's conversion had come during an interview with the Charlotte *Observer*, a two-hour marathon in which he and Maggie Ray were questioned at length about their differences and common ground. When the interview ended, and the reporters had drifted away, he and Maggie remained closeted in an editor's office, and the more they talked, the more certain they became that they could work well together. There was a personal affinity between them; Sanders had been Tom Ray's teacher back at Central High School, and in recent weeks, he had come to admire Maggie's serenity and intelligence, her graceful air of control, her firm and gentle guidance of a fractious committee. "If they let us do it," Sanders remembers saying near the end of their talk, "I believe we can work it out."

Maggie was genuinely excited about the prospect, but skeptical that the school board would really go along. It was true that Dick Spangler and Julia Maulden had defended the idea of compromise at the May 28 meeting, but their suggestions had received no response from the others and certainly not from Poe. By Friday, May 31, however, the mood of the board seemed to be very different. Julia Maulden repeated her plea for serious negotiation, and though no vote was taken, five other board members supported that suggestion. Bill Poe was one of the five. "From my standpoint," he declared, "if they [CAG members] could justify some of their conclusions, I'd be interested in a compromise."

What had happened?

Poe's shift was a mystery at the time, but in retrospect, the factors seem clear. First, there was the lingering possibility, even the likelihood, that in the absence of a compromise, Judge McMillan would simply side with the CAG. It was obvious that the judge had little sympathy or patience with the school board's plan, and a simple rejection of it would leave the board and the community with terrible choices. At least that was how Poe saw it. He still thought the CAG proposal was seriously flawed, and if McMillan ordered it implemented in the fall, the only alternative might be to appeal. Poe wasn't sure the community had the stomach for it—wasn't sure, in fact, that he had it himself. The pressure was building for a settlement of the issue ("peace in the valley," as W. T. Harris liked to put it), and some of the pressure now came from high places.

But as Ed Sanders and others who were close to him knew, Bill Poe was motivated by something else as well. He had sworn to preserve and protect the public schools of Charlotte-Mecklenburg, and the turmoil of the busing case was still tearing them apart. You could argue, of course, over whose fault that was, and Poe's inclination was to put the blame on the judge. But in a very important way, that didn't matter any more, for the simple truth was the turmoil was real, and there was no way to end it—no way to rescue the schools from their agony—without swallowing a little pride for the greater public good. Thus, when Ed Sanders—a man in whom Poe had great confidence—declared that he could work with Maggie Ray, the board chairman understood that the time had finally come. Though it pained him to do it, he gave Sanders his blessing. Go for it, he said. And Ed Sanders did.

Beginning in the first week of June, he and Maggie Ray met every morning in his office. Sanders was freed from all other duties and protected, more or less, from the ringing of the phone, and from 8:30 till lunchtime, they would pore over the maps and debate the larger principles. Maggie was unyielding on at least a few points. Whites from the southeast must go to West Charlotte, for in the mind of the community and in the mind of the judge, that had become the litmus test of good faith. It might have been irrational, more symbolic than it really should have been, but that was how it was, and Maggie would not budge, even when Sanders raised the specter of a new round of white flight. She also insisted that all students be bused at some point, and that those black students who were currently being bused for twelve years be assigned close to home for a minimum of three. Sanders slowly gave ground on those points; he knew that philosophically Maggie was probably right, and he knew also that she had some powerful allies, not the least of whom were W. T. Harris and Judge McMillan. But it was nevertheless true, he told her, that in some of its specifics the CAG plan was an amateurish nightmare. Under its calculations, some high schools would draw students from as many as eight junior highs, and that kind of fragmentation simply had to be corrected.

He found Maggie agreeable on those kinds of points, found her pleasant and reasonable no matter what the issue, and so they spent five weeks working out the details. Maggie reported each day to members of her committee, and Sanders, significantly, reported directly to Poe. Sanders had always admired the board chairman's tenacity, but during this period, he also came to admire his restraint and statesmanship. One day, for example, he and Maggie had agreed that there was no alternative to assigning children from Poe's own street (an old and winding avenue called Coniston Place, with handsome brick houses and a spreading canopy of oaks) to West Charlotte High School. With some trepidation, and with Maggie still in his office, Sanders telephoned Poe to give him the news. "Do it," Poe said, and that was all. The hurdle had been crossed, and Ed and Maggie knew that their effort would succeed.

W. T. Harris, meanwhile, smiled with satisfaction when he heard the news. He was immensely pleased, but not at all surprised. "Bill Poe," he said quietly, "has faced the hard leather and come up a man—just like we knew he would."

July 9, 1974, and July 11, 1975, were jubilant days in Charlotte. On the first, the school board formally approved the work of Ed and Maggie and voted to submit their joint proposal to Judge McMillan. The approval came as no surprise, for in addition to the private support of Bill Poe, there was reason to expect public backing from the board majority. Julia Maulden and Carlton Watkins had recently stepped aside at the end of their terms, but they had been replaced by two moderates: Marylyn Huff, who had run unsuccessfully in 1972, and John McLaughlin, a small-town postmaster from the northern part of the county. In addition, Sam McNinch, a hard-line conservative for most of his time on the board, had been defeated that summer in his bid for reelection, losing to Bob Culbertson, the strong public school activist from southeast Charlotte and a former member of the CAG.

Still, Ed and Maggie were nagged by doubts. They knew that Bill Booe was certain to oppose them, and they were not yet sure of Tom

Harris, one of the board's longtime opponents of busing. But Harris (who was no relation to W. T.) had been giving the issue careful thought. For some time now, he had impressed his board colleagues with his maturity and generosity—his willingness to speak his mind, but his determination also to be part of the team, to work for the good of the schools, and not hold them hostage to his own ideology. And on July 9, 1974, that was once again the path that he chose. He could not vote for Ed and Maggie's plan, he said. His principles would not allow it. But neither, Harris added, would he seek to "torpedo" it. He understood and respected the consensus of the board, and he would simply cast his vote without further dissent.

The next day, Judge McMillan offered his own approval to the plan, and a year and a day later, after watching with satisfaction the way it had worked, the judge announced that he was closing the Charlotte school case.

In a final order that he entitled "Swann Song," McMillan wrote: "This order intends . . . to close the file, to leave the constitutional operation of the schools to the board, which assumed that burden after the latest election; and to express again a deep appreciation to the board members, community leaders, school administrators, teachers and parents who have . . . made possible this court's graduation from Swann." Therefore, McMillan said, it was ordered "that the file be closed. This 11 day of July, 1975."

The relief and satisfaction that followed in Charlotte were hard to overstate, comparable, some said, to the feelings at the armistice of World War II. One commentator who caught the sense of the mood was a Charlotte *Observer* editorial writer by the name of Jack Claiborne. He celebrated the magnitude of the Charlotte accomplishment and tried to offer a sense of what had made it possible. It was, he argued, a classic case study in the workings of democracy—the powerful and mysterious swirl of ideas, the intertwining values offered up by the early black pioneers, the tenacious attorneys on both sides of the case, a courageous federal judge, and a strong-willed chairman of the board of education. But that was not all. There had been teachers, students, and parents and a handful of bureaucratic heroes in the school system's staff; and there

had been ordinary citizens, some of them liberal and others quite conservative, and there had been Old South politicians like W. T. Harris.
They had been compelled by circumstances to give it their best, and in
seeking to fathom what had happened as a result, Jack Claiborne was
soon thumbing through the writings of Tocqueville: "Democracy," the
French philosopher had declared in 1840, "does not provide a people
with the most skillful of governments, but it does that which the most
skillful government often cannot do: it spreads throughout the social
body a restless activity, superabundant force and energy never found
elsewhere, which, however little favored by circumstance, can do wonders. Those are its true advantages."

Ed Sanders understood the point, but in his own postmortem he
added something else. The experience, he said, had been not only a
triumph of democracy, but a triumph also of a sense of *community*. That
idea, Sanders explained, had come home to him at a party on the
occasion of his retirement, an event that occurred not long after the
settlement of the case. The celebration occurred at Maggie Ray's house,
and the guest list included, among others, Judge McMillan, Bill Poe,
W. T. Harris, Tom Harris, and young Phil Berry, the black school board
member who would take over as board chairman after Poe stepped
aside. Sanders was impressed not only by the diversity of the list, but by
the amiability of the gathering, despite all the pain that the community
had endured. Glancing across the room as the evening wound down, he
saw McMillan and Tom Harris in friendly conversation—the little federal judge and the former linebacker who once led the resistance to his
orders—and as they were talking, Harris had draped his arm across
McMillan's shoulders. Sanders remembers the lump that came to his
throat, and the idea that quickly formed in his mind: "That," he thought,
with a little nod of admiration, "says something good about this town."

The Aftermath

10

The Golden Decade

For a time at least, and in many different ways, the city was not the same.

Even before the final settlement of Darius Swann's lawsuit, the interracial coalition that had taken shape in Hampshire Hills had already expanded to other parts of town, and had begun embracing issues beyond the future of schools. David Frye, Julian Mason, and their other friends in north Charlotte were not alone in their perception that blacks and whites would do better as allies. A Methodist minister on the city's West Side, a white man of rural origins named Floyd Berrier, had moved to Charlotte in 1971, just about the time of the Supreme Court's *Swann* ruling, and he was struck immediately by the tense racial feelings. Antibusing sentiment abounded in his area, which was working-class, a former mill village called Thomasboro, full of small frame houses with aluminum sidings, and frightened white citizens who didn't want their children sent away to black areas. But that was not the only problem. Blacks were moving into the Thomasboro neighborhood, and whites were moving out, and Berrier thought the area might turn completely black. So he joined with a fellow Methodist minister, Ted Craddock, and a Presbyterian named Jeff Kesterman, in an effort to stem the tide of white flight.

In many ways, Berrier was particularly well suited to the role of activist, primarily because he didn't really seem like one. He was a stocky man, friendly, and easygoing, with a squarish face and a mustache that created the vague impression of a walrus. His speech was still heavy with a rural accent, and among the conservative white people of Charlotte's West Side, his manner and personality inspired a ready confidence. Armed with that confidence, and supported by his other friends in the West Side pulpits, Berrier helped form a group called the West Side Committee for Organization, with leaders carefully chosen for their lack of prejudice. Two of the most important were Sam Smith, an articulate, tactful; and polished businessman, and Marvin Smith, a blustery truck driver for Lance potato chips. The Smiths were not related, but they complemented each other perfectly, giving the WCO a grass-roots leadership that was earthy and shrewd. Those were heady times in the early and mid-1970s, when the Smiths and Floyd Berrier began to realize—and began to see the idea dawn on their friends—that the problems of working-class whites and the problems of blacks were remarkably the same: They all wanted to see a fairer busing plan. They all sought a greater voice in the councils of government. They all wanted more and better service from their local bureaucracy—greater protection against fires and urban crime, quicker response from the ambulance service. These were problems, of course, that knew no color, and Sam and Marvin Smith, like their mentors in the pulpit, saw hope and possibility in the forging of coalitions. By 1975, there was already growing cooperation between their organization and white neighborhood groups in other parts of town. The breakthrough came when they began to work with blacks.

Arguably, the most impressive of those was Ron Leeper, a young businessman who had grown up poor beyond the outskirts of Charlotte, and still remembered the visits of Klansmen in the night. Leeper, in those days, had a militant look, with his large Afro and Fu Manchu mustache, but he was poised and articulate and generous of spirit—a perfect match for Sam Smith, with whom he quickly developed an easy friendship.

It was no accident, Smith thought, that the West Side coalition of black and white activists came together firmly in 1975, for that was the year that the busing case was settled, and the climate in Charlotte was suddenly very different. The feeling was everywhere that the city had accomplished something rare in America. It had finally come to terms with the old problems of race, and the great American Dilemma, as Smith put it, "was something we just didn't have to bring up anymore."

Thus freed, he and his allies began to consider the possibility of a bold new strategy: a grass-roots campaign for a new form of city government, one that was fairer and more fully representative. Instead of a city council elected entirely at large and dominated (though there were several strong exceptions) by white businessmen from southeast Charlotte, they would seek some form of district representation, assuring a greater voice for black and white neighborhoods throughout the city. They presented the idea to the existing city council, and found two supporters: Harvey Gantt, a young black architect and civil rights pioneer, who had been the first black student at Clemson University; and Betty Chafin, an energetic young woman who was rapidly emerging as a neighborhood advocate. Unfortunately, Gantt and Chafin did not have the votes, and certainly, at that point, they lacked the clout of the city's mayor, John Belk, who frequently found himself on the wrong side of history. Belk had been disgraceful in his silence during the busing controversy, declaring at one point when a reporter asked about the schools: "That comes under the county budget, not under the city budget." And when it came to the subject of district representation, Belk's lack of vision was replaced by arrogance. He vetoed the idea.

But the proponents of it would not be silenced, for they were caught up now in the heady notion of equity, a pervasive new sense of what Charlotte was all about. Sam Smith and his allies knew that Mayor Belk was a good man in many ways, committed to a certain vision of what was best for his city, an orderly vision, really, involving neat and rather predictable decisions, made by people of proven good judgment: business people with a demonstrated knack for getting things done. Under his regime, however, the problems of the West Side had been allowed to fester, and Smith and other leaders were determined to be heard. The city, they declared, belonged to everyone, and its problems and opportunities were there to be shared. It was the same rhetoric, the same ideal, that had turned the busing case around, and between 1975 and 1977, it proved equally effective in the pursuit of district government. Working with Ron Leeper, and with other black leaders such as Bob Walton and L. C. Coleman, Smith and other whites devised a district plan that assured blacks at least two district seats out of seven, with the possibility of a third. The plan was supported by neighborhood leaders all over Charlotte, and working door-to-door in 1977, they gathered more than five thousand signatures on a petition to force a referendum.

The vote was held on April 19, 1977, and the proponents of districts, having spent a grand total of $476 for their whole campaign, won by eighty votes.

The victory produced in Charlotte a far more diverse and representative city government. The city council included, by 1985, six women and five men, six Democrats and five Republicans, and they made absolutely certain that every important agency, board, or commission involved in local government was racially integrated and geographically diverse. For, as one local business leader put it: "You can't have a community unless it works for everybody." That view continued to spread in the late seventies and early eighties, informing the public debate on a variety of issues. Dennis Rash, for example, felt it keenly when the bank at which he worked, North Carolina National Bank, became involved in the effort to rebuild the central city—not only to modernize it as a center of commerce, but to restore its fading residential areas. It began with a once-grand neighborhood known as Fourth Ward, with Victorian houses in contagious disrepair, their porches sagging, their paint chipping away with the passage of the years. There was, nevertheless, a lingering nostalgia about the Fourth Ward area, an aura of old ghosts from the turn of the century. With an infusion of bank money for rehabilitation, and for the construction of town houses in the style of old Charleston, they began to lure affluent families back to downtown.

"It would never have happened without the busing case," Rash argues, and the first reason for that was practical and obvious. White families and those of the black gentry would never have returned to the inner city if the only educational options for their children had been neighborhood schools: underfunded facilities near crowded public housing, where most of the students were black and very poor. Because of busing, that was no longer the case. The closest schools to downtown were Irwin Avenue and First Ward Elementary, both now populated with an eclectic mix of students.

But Dennis Rash was convinced that there was something else at work in the restoration of downtown—a diminution, he believed, in the fear of the unknown, a growing feeling among whites that they could live peacefully in the presence of blacks. So in 1980, Rash set out to test

that theory more directly even than he had in Fourth Ward. Working
with city officials and with neighborhood leaders in a predominantly
black area known as Third Ward, he led the effort by North Carolina
National Bank to develop an integrated Third Ward community with
residents from a variety of economic backgrounds.

"There wasn't any nostalgia about Third Ward," he remembers. "It
was a lower-middle-class black neighborhood with a scrapyard for a
neighbor. But we set out to build a racially and economically integrated
neighborhood—and we pulled it off. That says a whole lot about the
changes in the city."

Rash was not alone in that feeling. Harvey Gantt, the black city
councilman, was elected Charlotte's mayor in 1983 and again in 1985,
winning 60 percent of the vote in his bid for reelection, even though
more than 75 percent of Charlotte's voters were white. It was, he
thought, a culmination of changes that began with busing and continued
through the push for district representation. W. T. Harris agreed. In
1984, when a study commission from the National Education Association prepared a report on integration successes, Harris told them: "As
you know, we elected a black mayor the other day, and we are proud of
him. He is a fine man. He is going to lead us. I would say to you that
prior to school integration, we couldn't have done that, regardless of
how good he was. We have grown tremendously."

Nevertheless, there were still some serious problems confronting the
public schools. In 1976, for example, shortly after the closing of the
Swann lawsuit, there was another important piece of unfinished business, another ugly item on the school board's agenda.

The superintendent since 1972, when Bill Self left to become a dean
at the University of North Carolina, had been a tall and scholarly man
named Rolland Jones. There was no doubt that Jones was a talented
educator. He had come with good credentials from Edmonton, Alberta,
and he had looked forward to the challenge of the Charlotte situation.
During the campus uprisings that continued through the spring of 1973,
the vicious, often bloody standoffs between young blacks and whites,
Jones proved a calm and steadying force. His voice was soft and firm
and reassuring, and when he addressed student assemblies at racially

troubled high schools, or talked to the whole community on public television, he was clear about the virtues of black and white together. "Desegregation is the law," he declared more than once, "and integration is a proper goal."

There was no doubt that the schools improved during Jones's tenure, for that was the time when they rode out the storm—when the uprisings abated, when white flight slowed to barely a trickle, and when, after dipping initially, student test scores began to go up. Jones embraced integration more completely and forthrightly than any of his predecessors, and he began the massive training of teachers to cope with its effects. But there were ways in which Jones was disturbingly ineffective. If, as Bill Self liked to say, there were two kinds of superintendents—those who faced outward and engaged the whole community with their charisma and their charm and their political skills and those who faced inward to administer the schools—Jones somehow managed to be neither. His administrative staff found him distant and enigmatic, committed, for example, to the *principle* of desegregation, but aloof from the details of the pupil assignment plan. And even more significantly, the city's business and political leadership came quickly to regard the superintendent with contempt. He was just not a man who could speak their language. He was shy, for one thing, uncomfortable with the back-slapping of Southern politicians, inept at the subtleties of their kind of diplomacy. So the impression began to grow within the local leadership that Rolland Jones was not a man to be trusted: he was awkward and even disdainful, it seemed, yet irritatingly verbose once you finally got him talking. "Ask the man a simple question," groused W. T. Harris, "and he would give you an answer that would take twenty minutes." So as chairman of the board of county commissioners, the agency that controlled the school system's purse strings, Harris went to his friend Dick Spangler on the board of education and told him sometime during 1975, "If you don't get rid of this fool, you ain't gonna get any more money."

Spangler had been a staunch public supporter of Jones, and he didn't take the statement as a literal threat. But he saw it as one more symptom of a problem getting worse, and when Jones became an issue, serious and divisive, during the 1976 school board election, Spangler decided that the time had come to act. "This was not long after the closing of the *Swann* case," he remembers, still wincing slightly, as if the pain of the decision remains near the surface. "The school system was still in the recovery room after a critical operation. I decided we had to eliminate Jones, so that the new school board, instead of becoming divided over his future, could become united in selecting his successor." Thus, at a school board meeting on August 18, 1976, Spangler moved that Jones be fired, and by a vote of six to one, with one abstention, the board passed the motion. Jones was shattered by the suddenness (though he landed on his feet, as superintendent of schools in a Long Island town), and for many people in Charlotte, the firing was another nasty wound. But the school system survived, led for more than a year by three stalwart administrators—John Phillips, Chris Folk, and a respected black woman named Elizabeth Randolph; and when the school board finally selected a permanent successor, the choice was one of the wisest that the board ever made. Jay Robinson's superintendency would assure, at least for a while, that the community would hold fast to the course that it had chosen.

Robinson was not at all a likely champion of integration. In many ways, he was the antithesis of Rolland Jones. Instead of coming to Charlotte from a large school system in a faraway place, he had spent more than a quarter century in the county next door. He had begun as a coach in 1950 (his basketball team at Odell School lost only ten games in the seven years he coached it), and he had made his way through the ranks of coaching and teaching, becoming Cabarrus County's superintendent in 1965. He was almost the stereotype of the small-town educator, tall and gangly, with a friendly and eager Walter Matthau face, and a twangy mountain accent exquisitely preserved. If Rolland Jones had tended to speak in educationese, Jay Robinson, in the words of W. T. Harris, "butchered the king's English about as bad as I do."

Those things would prove important when he was offered the Charlotte superintendency, but the indispensable ingredient in the success that awaited him, the thing that set him apart from ordinary superintendents, was the ardor of his commitment to desegregation. Not even Julius Chambers was a more devoted advocate, which struck some people as strange, given Robinson's background. He came from the small town of Bandana, in mountainous Mitchell County, North Carolina, where the number of black people could be counted on your fingers. For the first fifteen years of his career, he had never worked at a single school that had a black student. But one fall afternoon in 1964, Robinson, then assistant superintendent of schools in Cabarrus County, paid an afternoon visit to a football practice. He struck up a conversation with a young boy in pads, a bright, good-looking young man, who was the first and only black student at his school. The boy was not frightened by the role of pioneer. But on this particular afternoon, he was quiet and sober and a little bit depressed, and he told the assistant superintendent, the lanky white man with the deep Southern drawl: "I can't play football here. Just look. I'm the only one like me."

Robinson immediately began reflecting on the ironies of the times, the pain and the loneliness of the isolated blacks, the energy being expended to preserve the status quo. Segregation was wrong. That was already clear. But token integration—that halfhearted assault on the barriers of the past—was both pointless and cruel, and the time had now arrived for something more drastic.

Such anecdotal reflections were characteristic of Robinson. Though he had a master's degree from the University of North Carolina and a Ph.D. from Duke, his most deeply held beliefs did not come from books. They came from people, whom he observed with a rare combination of shrewdness and sentiment. Thus, the black boy in the pads at the Winecoff School set off passionate ruminations that led to new certainties; and when Robinson was named Cabarrus County's superintendent in 1965, his first major recommendation, which came only a month after he accepted the job, was for the total integration of the county's public schools.

It happened the next fall, but not without some trouble. There was an active Ku Klux Klan in Cabarrus County, with headquarters four blocks from where Robinson lived. His life was threatened repeatedly by callers in the night. Black teachers were harassed, and their homes became the target of terrorists' bullets. Still, the system survived, and so did Jay Robinson, and with the integration issue now thoroughly settled, the county's resources, both financial and emotional, became focused more fully on the task of education.

The challenge in Charlotte was different, of course. When Robinson was offered that job in 1977, the necessity was not to accomplish integration, but to try to preserve it. And if there were new delicacies and complexities involved in that effort, the superintendent soon discovered some powerful allies. Arguably the most important were the Charlotte-Mecklenburg teachers. Some were mediocre, there was no doubt about it, but overall, Robinson could scarcely believe the quality and commitment of many he inherited. There was Mertye Rice, for example, a tiny black woman at West Charlotte High School, who, in a public presentation near the end of her career, offered this soliloquy on the nature of her calling: "Forty-three years lugging a sack full of books, magazines, corrected papers, breakfast, lunch. Waiting for the eager faces to come through the door—well, some eager, some not quite so eager; we could tell by the expressions what kind of day it was going to be. But with a lot of patience, love, understanding, sometimes protection, we could make it." Miss Rice seemed to make no distinctions, in her affectionate recollections, between her most brilliant students at West Charlotte High School and those of lesser talent, who could barely read. And certainly, though the school was all black for most of her time there, she made no racial distinctions once the white students arrived. "She was maybe the only black teacher I know," recalls Elizabeth Randolph, Miss Rice's close friend who worked in the system's administration, "who never encountered any problems in her dealings with white students. Students were students, and all of them were precious, and they could sense immediately that she felt that way. She could walk up to two students who were fighting, and without raising her voice, sometimes without even speaking, she could give them a look that said, 'Now boys, this is not how you want to behave.' And they would stop. They couldn't resist the sheer force of her caring. She was one of a kind." Miss Rice, however, did not see it that way. In her own estimation, she was not one of a kind, but part of a team: one of literally hundreds of Charlotte-Mecklenburg teachers, black and white, who were almost ferocious in their commitment to the goal of integration. And after the hard early years of tension and violence, she became, in 1974, one of the central players in a heralded event—a triumphant proclamation, noted with awe by the national news media, that whatever the problems of the past, integration in Charlotte was now a success. Some West Charlotte students had been reading the headlines then coming out of Boston, the depressing catalogues of carnage that went beyond anything that had happened in Charlotte: white adults stoning buses that were filled with black children, black gangs roaming the streets of Roxbury, school campuses surrounded by riot-trained police. The students were not smug in making their comparisons. They knew that the differences were small matters of degree, that Charlotte, too, had skated to the edge of deadly trouble, but that peace was possible on the other side of those times. Thus, in early October, Tina Gouge, a West Charlotte junior, was struck with a deceptively simple idea: why not write letters of encouragement to their Boston counterparts? She mentioned the possibility to a few of her friends, and with the support of teachers like Mertye Rice, and West Charlotte's new principal, Sam Haywood, nine students crafted letters of a few paragraphs, all of which were printed in the Boston *Globe*.

"I hope you people will have the patience and determination to make a go of the situation you are in," wrote Tina Gouge. "We, here in Charlotte, have faith in you and care about what is happening to you."

The simplicity of the sentiment drew national attention, with the added twist that it was man-bites-dog: students from the South, where the morality play of race had so long dominated the national headlines, setting an example for their counterparts in the liberal northeast. But it was not an accident, or an inexplicable aberration. For years, under superintendents William Self and Rolland Jones, the school system had worked hard at the business of human relations—not only in response to the sudden eruptions of crisis, but in an ongoing program of student seminars and workshops, coordinated by the National Conference of Christians and Jews. The NCCJ's Charlotte director, Kitty Huffman, was convinced that students and teachers, perhaps even more than parents and politicians, held the key to progress, and she was intensely proud of the students at West Charlotte. Their letter writing quickly grew to something more ambitious—an exchange of student visits between Charlotte and Boston, which Mrs. Huffman and Mertye Rice helped organize. Their efforts became part of a new Charlotte mythology, a ten-year period of national publicity as the City That Made It Work.

There were more headlines in 1976 and 1977, after a proposal to transform Northwest Junior High (an ugly assemblage of faded brick buildings, where the whites were bused in from the former mill town of Thomasboro) into an experimental facility with a new student body. School officials were stunned at the response. More than two hundred students began circulating a petition, pleading with officials to leave Northwest alone. They were happy there, the students said. The gesture was astonishing not only because most of the petition-signers were working-class whites, but because their parents, only a few years earlier, had been circulating petitions for precisely the opposite reason— demanding an end to the busing of their children, seeking their reassignment from Northwest Junior High.

"At one time we looked at people as being black or white," said Kelly Edwards, a soft-eyed eighth-grader, as she presented the students' petition to the school board. "But now we have a real good time just because we're friends. I hope ya'll on the board won't take that away from us." Kelly's father, Jack Edwards, sat stiffly in the audience, occasionally averting his eyes to stare at his shoes. He remembered the scenes from five years before, how Kelly's older sister had been injured in a race riot, and how he had screamed as loudly as anyone that busing was insane. "It was rough in the beginning," he said, as Kelly finished her speech. "But Kelly and these kids have pulled it off."

Jay Robinson was proud of such stories, and he knew there were others. Lee Hogewood, an honors student at Harvard and the son of school board member Ashley Hogewood, had begun first grade during the first year of busing. He was a student at Billingsville Elementary, where principal Kathleen Crosby led the struggle to achieve integration. When Lee got to Harvard, he discovered several things: First, he had gotten a superb education in the Charlotte public schools, one that enabled him to compete in the Ivy League. He knew that not all his Charlotte classmates could say the same thing; there were students, black and white, who had fallen through the cracks. But Lee saw no reason to dispute his family's view that integration held the key to better things. Thus, at Harvard, he took perverse satisfaction in the dormitory conversations, particularly the animated exchanges with students from the North, who were incredulous at first, and then a little envious, of the unlikely achievement of a community from the South. "Yeah, I guess I was proud," he said, looking back; and he decided to write his senior thesis on the Charlotte-Mecklenburg experience—125 pages on the brave struggles of his city.

Jay Robinson knew there were thousands of students with the attitudes of Lee Hogewood or Kelly Edwards and hundreds of teachers with the dedication of Mertye Rice. Nevertheless, he was nervous about the city's occasional lapses into self-congratulation. He knew there was social resegregation in many of the schools. High school students, in particular, were grouping themselves by race in the cafeterias and playgrounds, despite all the efforts to achieve integration. He knew also there were large numbers of former students—he was never sure how many—who still shared their parents' distaste for the busing experiment, having come away embittered by the early years of turmoil. Robinson feared new problems could well lie ahead.

June 20, 1978, was a bad day for him, one of the worst he would have as Charlotte's superintendent. At noon, he received the results of the state competency tests, new computerized exams for high school students, which the students had to pass before they could graduate. The 1978 scores were less important than the ones that would follow. The testing program was in its first experimental year, and any students who failed would receive another chance. But the scores were appalling. More than eighty percent of the black juniors who took the tests, twice the number of whites, failed either the math or the reading components, which meant they lacked skills they should have acquired in elementary school.

Robinson understood immediately the implications of those facts. First and most obviously, the schools were still failing the majority of black students, or at least that majority in the upper grades whose educations had begun before desegregation was complete. "It makes you sick," he told his staff, and he told the same thing to reporters who descended on his office. He knew that black test scores in the days of dual schools had been used by Julius Chambers to buttress the case for integration. But now, after eight years of busing, eighty percent of the black juniors in Charlotte's high schools were not yet minimally competent in reading or math. At least that was the indication from the first round of tests, and the question now was whether segregationists would seize on such numbers to launch a new offensive.

Well, maybe they would, but the offensive would fail if the schools outflanked it. So Robinson called his executive staff together, and he made it clear what he expected them to do. There would be no excuses or doubletalk, he said, no evasion of the principle of the schools' accountability. The results were intolerable, and within a year they would change. Even taking into account the economic factors, those terrible deprivations of culture and values that still afflicted so many black families, it was simply inconceivable that blacks couldn't do better. The problem was simple in its broadest sense: There were still— after all the turmoil and noble hopes of desegregation—too many students who were not being taught. The schools were failing, and that had to change, but the change needn't be softheaded or mushy. For those high school students who were not yet competent, there had to be a massive remedial program, one-to-one almost, to provide them the skills they had missed along the way. There would be charges, he knew, that they were teaching the test—and indeed they would be teaching *to* the test, but that was all right, for the test measured things that competent people had to know. But the remedial program was a bandaid, he said, or maybe the stitching against a hemorrhage of credibility. The larger need was to "get the kids to come to school, to behave themselves and to study their lessons. If you can do those three things, you've pretty much got the problems solved." So that was what Robinson set out to do. He ordered tough new emphasis on attendance and discipline: no gang fighting, no selling of drugs, no weapons on campus, no assaults on teachers. Expulsion was automatic for any of those offenses. Nor was promotion from one grade to the next a given anymore. There would be standardized tests in the third, sixth, and ninth grades, with minimum requirements before the students moved on.

Those programs, concrete and understandable, gave substance to a style that went beyond what was tangible. There was something undeniable about Robinson's hillbilly passion—a force of personality that rippled through the bureaucracy and sent an urgent message all the way to the classroom. His predecessor, Rolland Jones, had been an inspiration to the best teachers in the system, for he projected strong support for creative innovation. Robinson did not want to lose that, but he was concerned not only about allowing Mertye Rice and the other superstars to perform at their best. He knew that hundreds of other teachers, the majority in fact, were simply not as good, but they too were indispensable to the functioning of the system. So Robinson worked on articulating the minimums—bottom-line expectations that every teacher had to meet: Get the students to class. Make them behave. Try to make sure that they study their lessons.

For the most part, it worked. Student test scores (not a full measure of quality, he knew, but probably the best one that the schools had available) soon began an accelerating climb. The upward trend had begun before Robinson arrived, but the scores in those days were still not encouraging. Even in 1978, on the California Achievement Test, black third graders were reading in the nineteenth percentile (thirty-one points below the national average), and the same was roughly true of sixth and ninth graders. Black math scores were barely any better, but between 1978 and 1986 when the tests were renormed, there were dramatic improvements every year. Black third graders jumped from the twentieth percentile to the forty-eighth on the total battery of math and reading tests; black sixth graders rose from the twenty-second to the fiftieth, precisely the national average, and black ninth graders from the twentieth to the forty-sixth. White scores climbed impressively as well, not quite as rapidly as the blacks', but by 1985 they were thirty points above the national average. "It would never have happened," declares Chris Folk, a veteran of more than thirty years in the Charlotte-Mecklenburg system, "absolutely would never have happened without integration."

Jay Robinson agreed, and for a time such results, in combination with his style and diplomatic skills, gave him a credibility among the people of Charlotte that was virtually carte blanche. He did not expect that situation to last, but while it did he was determined to use it, for there were difficult decisions that had to be made. The most troubling question was whether to allow the first movement toward resegregation, for in 1978, less than three years after the closing of the Charlotte-Mecklenburg case, population shifts were starting to exert a strain. Charlotte as a city was growing quite rapidly (its metropolitan area would soon reach a million people), and almost suddenly, there were vast concentrations of affluent white people living on the fringes of southeast Charlotte. Many were new arrivals who had little appreciation for the community's recent achievements. They simply wanted their children to go to good schools, and preferably good schools that were close to their homes.

Outside the southeast, meanwhile, there had been other demographic changes in the city, shifting concentrations of white and black populations that were tearing at the ratios of a dozen different schools. It was now clear to Robinson, if indeed he ever doubted it, that the old and much talked about goal of stability had not been achieved, and might never be. The question was what to do about it. In the old days, of course, it would have been a question for the courts, something to be decided by Judge McMillan and grudgingly implemented by a reluctant school board. But no longer. The Supreme Court had been clear in its 1971 ruling: "Neither school authorities nor district courts are constitutionally *required* to make year-by-year adjustments of the racial compositions of their student bodies once the affirmative duty to desegregate has been accomplished." But neither did the court *prohibit* such adjustments: "School authorities are traditionally charged with broad power to formulate and implement educational policy and might well conclude, for example, that in order to prepare students to live in a pluralistic society each school should have a prescribed ratio of Negro to white students. . . . To do this as an educational policy is within the broad discretionary powers of school authorities."

So there it was. It was up to Jay Robinson, and it was up to the board—and ultimately, of course, it was up to the people. There was no longer a court order behind which to hide. Would they preserve integration, or would they let it slip away?

Robinson's own answer was quick and emphatic. Neighborhood schools were an appealing idea—convenient and reassuring, even natural somehow. But the major problem with them was also obvious: they reflected their neighborhoods. Good neighborhoods tended to have good schools, but bad neighborhoods, where drugs and crime and destructive habits were abundant, were almost certain to have bad schools. That, however, was no longer the case in Charlotte. The old insistence on *fairness*—that instinctive outcry of Julian Mason and

David Frye, of Judge McMillan and the CAG—had begun to pay a dividend that they hadn't foreseen. It had brought about an economic integration of the public schools, a sprinkling of middle-class and wealthy students through much of the system, and they had now become the great leavening force. Their presence brought added resources to their schools—more parental involvement, more money to provide the crucial extras (supplemental texts and library books, maps, globes, film strips, sometimes new sets of encyclopedias) that bore directly on the quality of learning.

There was another argument, too, that Jay Robinson used, for it concerned what he saw as a frightening possibility. Based on the experiences of Nashville, Memphis, and other comparable-sized cities, it appeared that white flight *accelerated* with resegregation. The reason for that was easy enough to grasp. Whites tended to flee from schools that passed a tipping point and became too black, and cities which allowed that to happen could expect to pay a price. In Charlotte, however, the black ratio was stable. It had risen by a percentage point a year—from twenty-nine percent to thirty-seven percent—between 1968 and 1977. But now the increase had leveled off and it would take three years for the ratio to reach thirty-eight percent, and another three to reach thirty-nine percent. Robinson didn't want to tamper with the stability, and the best way to preserve it, he argued, was to maintain the status quo in desegregation.

He found willing allies on the board of education. Bill Poe was gone; in 1976, after a decade in the trenches, he had decided not to run for reelection. He had been replaced as chairman, first by Phil Berry, and later by Carrie Winter, a reflective, somewhat low-key woman, who had served on Maggie Ray's committee and was a courageous believer in the necessity of integration. Throughout the late seventies and early eighties, most of the board had similar credentials: Betsy Bennett had been Maggie Ray's cochairman on the CAG; Ward McKeithen and Ashley Hogewood, two white attorneys, had supported integration at Billingsville Elementary; Sarah Stephenson had been the first black president of the integrated council of PTAS; and George Battle, a black minister, was color-blind in his commitment to the education of all children. A good group, Jay Robinson thought. And they were willing to do their duty

even when it was hard. Thus, at Robinson's urging, in 1978 they voted
to reassign 5,810 students to prevent resegregation, and for seven of the
next eight years, despite parental protests, they moved anywhere from
805 to more than 2,000 students.

"I know it's hard," Robinson declared a little wistfully, "but it'll take
another fifteen or twenty years to really make progress. If we stay the
course for the rest of this century, stay in there, it will be so obvious how
far we have come, you'd never retreat."

If for a time nearly everyone believed him, or so it came to seem, that
was never a reality Jay Robinson took for granted. As one of his
administrative colleagues put it: "Jay isn't the type who sits by and says
everything's going great. He gets up every morning and wonders, 'Is
the bubble going to burst today?' And every night when he goes to bed,
he says, 'Thank you, God. It didn't burst today.'"

11

The Unanswered Questions

The president was always such a sunny presence, and Jay Robinson watched him with grudging admiration. It was October 8, 1984. Robinson, a lifelong Democrat and no fan of Ronald Reagan's, would not ordinarily have switched on his television in the middle of a workday, just to catch a glimpse of a campaign speech. But word had come from reporters who had seen a text that on a stop that day at a Charlotte shopping mall, Reagan planned to speak out on the failure of busing. Robinson had trouble believing the report—had trouble believing that even Reagan could be that wrong, that insensitive, that misinformed. But sure enough. Staring out at the sea of white faces, in a place where integration was the proudest achievement of the century, the president had harsh words for the agenda of the Democrats. These, he said, were people who favored "busing that takes innocent children out of the neighborhood school and makes them pawns in a social experiment that nobody wants. And we've found out that it failed."

"That son of a bitch," Jay Robinson said, and he stalked across the room and switched off the TV.

Robinson was not a man who suffered fools gladly, nor was he known for his tolerance of those who opposed him, particularly on matters he regarded as important, and busing certainly fell into that category. Ever since his days in Cabarrus County, he had staked his career on the notion that integration—which, of course, was impossible to achieve without busing—was the only sensible option for most modern schools. It tended to equalize the educational resources, for when you put middle- and upper-class parents in nearly every school in the system, they simply insisted that those schools function well. The evidence was overwhelming that that had happened in Charlotte. Test scores were good, and generally getting better, and nobody doubted the intangible advances—those changes in mood and racial climate which, in the words of one prominent superintendent in New England, "made Charlotte-Mecklenburg synonymous with trying to do what's right." While Robinson appreciated that kind of praise, and had grown accustomed to it, he was also uneasy at the sense of isolation. He knew that Charlotte was not alone in its achievements. Success was equally obvious next door in Cabarrus County, or across the country in Seattle or Austin. But he felt himself swimming against a tide of national perception, for busing, it seemed, had been largely discredited by the failures of other cities.

The most celebrated of those failures had occurred in Boston, where, in 1974, U.S. District Judge Arthur Garrity had ruled that the city's schools were deliberately segregated. It was a strange and shameful irony in a place so identified with the ideals of freedom, a place where the abolitionist movement had once been headquartered. But before Judge Garrity could devise a remedy for it, he was doomed to basic failure by a set of legal precedents that had begun in other places, that traced, ironically, to the storied old court of another distinguished judge, Robert J. Mehrige of Richmond, Virginia.

Judge Mehrige was a Yankee by birth but a Southerner at heart, for after a successful career as a Richmond trial lawyer, he had ascended to the federal bench in 1967. With gratitude and courage, he had joined that tradition of activist Southern jurists, whose dean and founder was J. Waties Waring of Charleston. It was Waring who had accepted the old Clarendon County case in South Carolina, the first frontal assault on the segregation of schools, which had become part of the *Brown* decision of 1954. Since that time, federal judges in the South had been called to pass judgment on nearly every conceivable aspect of Southern life and culture, from voting rights to school segregation, from police brutality to the segregation of city buses. Judge Mehrige was no exception.

About the time of the Supreme Court ruling affirming Judge McMillan, Mehrige had issued an order in a case that would prove to be the most controversial, and in the end, the most disappointing, of any he had handled. It was a desegregation suit involving the Richmond public schools, and Mehrige sought to carry the logic of *Swann* a major step further. He ruled that busing was permissible across school district lines—across those geographic and political abstractions that separated Richmond city schools from the heavily white suburban districts that provided safe havens for Richmond's upper classes.

The ruling was important for many cities in the North, for places like Boston, Detroit, or Indianapolis, where inner-city schools were carefully set apart from predominantly white suburban systems that wanted no part of total integration. Court watchers and proponents of desegregation knew that in many cases, Northern integration would hinge on the Supreme Court's response to the Mehrige ruling.

For his own part, Mehrige was sure he was on firm legal ground. He had handled more than forty school desegregation cases, and it seemed to him a short and easy step from those rulings to the decision he reached in the Richmond case—that if the existence of suburban school systems, with their heavy white ratios, made it impossible to integrate the whole Richmond area, then busing between the suburbs and the city was a necessary step. But in 1972, the Supreme Court reversed him, signaling a new mood among the justices that this business of busing may be going too far. There was still a hint of doubt about the court's final stand, for the justices were split, and Lewis Powell, a Virginian, had excused himself from the Richmond ruling. But in the 1974 case of *Milliken* v. *Bradley*, a school desegregation suit from Detroit, Powell joined the majority against cross-district busing and thus sealed the doom of integration in Boston.

Segregation had been cleverly institutionalized in that historic city. The Boston school committee had practiced de jure apartheid, keeping white and black schools as separate as possible. But most whites of privilege were outside the practice, for their children were safe in suburban school districts legally distinct from the school system of the city. That left Judge Garrity with few decent choices. He could defend the constitutional principle of desegregation—and did, with courage and tenacity—but the results were dismal for the people of Boston. Educationally, it made little sense to transport poor blacks and less affluent whites back and forth from South Boston to Roxbury, which was about the only option that Garrity could order. The practice only served to embitter both races, and eleven years later, when the judge relinquished jurisdiction in the case, white enrollment in Boston had dropped to twenty-seven percent, down from fifty-two percent in 1974.

J. Anthony Lukas, whose brilliant book *Common Ground* tells the Boston story, sums up the city's experiences this way: "From the beginning Garrity's orders have labored under the liability of their essential class bias. Because Boston is the smallest major American city in relation to its metropolitan hinterland, few of the powerful, wealthy or privileged, and relatively few even of the solid middle class, live within the city's boundaries. . . . Only on historic Beacon Hill, in the elegant Back Bay and in the newly gentrified South End does one find the upper-income citizens who could provide some class leaven to the schools. This presented opponents of desegregation with a powerful issue of equity."

The opponents knew, says Lukas, that they were being compelled to bear a burden not imposed on Boston's wealthy suburbs, and it was a sense of injustice they shared for a while with their counterparts in Charlotte. There too, in the beginning, the most affluent areas were at least partially sheltered, as the school board, fearing white flight by those who could afford it (and perhaps also, wanting to protect their own children), chose to minimize the busing of wealthy white students. The early inconvenience thus tended to fall most heavily on blacks and on whites of lesser means. The difference was that Charlotte could do something about it. When David Frye and Julian Mason raised the issue of equity, Judge McMillan was free to respond. He was able to order major alterations in the school board's plan—a fairer distribution of the burdens and opportunities that went with integration. Charlotte-Mecklenburg operated one consolidated system, unencumbered by the hodge-podge of suburban school districts that shackled the city of Boston and doomed its children to unequal education. In Charlotte, cries for fairness became part of the solution. In Boston, thanks to Supreme Court rulings in Richmond and Detroit, those cries were simply one more refrain in a bitter litany of resistance.

The thing that troubled Jay Robinson was that Boston, not Charlotte, seemed to dominate the national perception. He was afraid that it was only a matter of time, and not much time, before that perception took its toll on the Charlotte consensus, before the city was confronted once again with organized resistance. Jay Robinson was right.

Not long after President Reagan's visit, a Charlotte lawyer named Ralph McMillan, a personable young conservative who was no relation to the judge, wrote an antibusing article for the *Wall Street Journal*, debunking the notion of Charlotte's great success. A new Republican legislator by the name of Ray Warren called for a public referendum on the subject of busing, and a failed Congressional candidate, Carl Horn III, wrote a guest column for the Charlotte *Observer*, once again arguing that busing was wrong. These were impressive young men, all highly intelligent and all genuinely offended by the notion of racism. They represented the cutting edge of Charlotte's New Right, and thus were all potential threats to Jay Robinson's leadership. Still, they were not the people that Robinson most feared. He knew that busing was not high on their agenda; Carl Horn was more interested in sex education, and Ray Warren, who had been bused himself to Independence High School, was clearly no proponent of resegregation. The New Right's opposition was largely abstract, principled and genuine, but it lacked that passion—that feeling of deep and personalized offense—the city had known in other times. Thus, Jay Robinson was far more concerned by another source of dissent, a neighborhood movement out in southeast Charlotte, led by a forty-ish salesman whose name was David Scheick.

Scheick was new to Charlotte. He had moved down from Indiana in 1978, and had bought a $70,000 house in Sardis Forest, a fresh new subdivision just beyond the city limits. Scheick liked the area. It was convenient to the school his two children would attend, and it was racially integrated, with at least one black family on virtually every street, and a smattering also of Koreans and other Asians. "A little United Nations," Scheick often called it, and he was happy to be there. But then in January of 1986, the peaceful world of Sardis Forest was suddenly disrupted. Jay Robinson proposed transferring 185 Sardis Forest children from nearby Matthews Elementary, which was overcrowded, to two other schools with rising black ratios. One of those schools, First Ward Elementary, was in the inner city, forty-five minutes away by bus, and it was located next to a black housing project. To some white parents, that location was disturbing, but not to Dave Scheick. He knew First Ward's reputation as an outstanding school, a case study in the benefits of desegregation, and except for the inconvenience, he didn't mind his children going there. But it was the *principle* of the thing, he told his wife Sandy. They had plunged into the life of Matthews Elementary and were now copresidents of the PTA. Matthews was integrated. Their neighborhood was integrated, and all of that was working well. Now, however, it was about to be disrupted. And why? So that somebody's racial ratios could be preserved temporarily—and the accent was on the word "temporarily." It would be one thing if the sacrifice being demanded of Sardis Forest would really mean something, if it really represented the solution to a problem. But at most it was only a stopgap measure, and all you had to do to prove the point was to look at recent history. Every year they were reassigning thousands of local children: more than 3,000 in 1983, nearly 1,700 in 1984, then 1,900 in 1985, and in 1986 more than 2,400. What kind of stability was that? What kind of long-range planning? There simply had to be a better way, and it was time for somebody to raise that question.

So the Scheicks began attending some neighborhood meetings, and they did their best to set the proper tone. Like Tom Harris at the founding of the old CPA, they were certain in their hearts that the issue wasn't racial. It was important to make that clear, they said, and it was important also to cast no aspersions on First Ward Elementary or doubt on the virtues of desegregation. The issue for their neighborhood was one of convenience and safety for their children on a long bus ride. For the whole community, the issue was good planning.

But if that was the way Scheick saw it, and if he defended the idea like the gentleman that he was, he was nevertheless swimming against the tide of recent history. Perhaps the most poignant reminder of that fact came shortly before the school board met on February 11 to consider Jay Robinson's reassignment proposals. The Sardis Forest parents were circulating a petition among their neighbors, and two of those parents, in the normal course of their rounds, came to 413 Morning Dale Road. It was a handsome house, part brick and part wood, set back from the road in a little grove of oak and cedar. They rang the bell, and a striking black woman met them at the door. She was tall and poised, with light brown skin and closely cropped hair that showed just a touch of gray. She read their petition, and then told them quietly: "No, I cannot sign this," and after a short pause: "This is not something that I believe in."

The woman was Dorothy Counts.

She felt a little sadness as the white parents left. They had asked for no explanation, and she had offered none. But later, when she told her husband Pete Scoggins of the petition and the visit, he scolded her gently and said, "That was your opportunity."

"Yes," she replied, "sometimes I don't think as fast on my feet as you do." Then Dorothy began to ask herself what she should have said—how she could have bridged that enormous gap of perception and history, to say nothing of race, that still shaped her relations with the people around her. Could she have made them see? Could she have talked about those days in 1957, when she had walked through the mobs at Harding High School, and Gus Roberts had done the same at Central, and how, because of that sacrifice and the thousands of others in the intervening years—not only by blacks, but by committed whites as well—how all of that had changed the city so profoundly for the better?

Her own children were now in public schools, happy with their friends, who were likely to be white, and her nephew was a student at Irwin Avenue Open School, an innovative, integrated elementary that occupied the building that had once been Harding. You could never have foreseen such things in 1957, and certainly could never have even dreamed that a neighborhood as fine as Sardis Forest would one day welcome all shades of people. She knew these things had not just happened. They were the result of effort and sacrifice and extreme inconvenience—precisely the sorts of things that these petition signers were seeking to avoid.

"Somebody has to do it." That's what Dorothy Counts had wanted to tell them, and she was not alone. When the Sardis Forest parents came before the school board, they hit a stone wall. The board was dominated by people like Sarah Stephenson, who had endured astonishing hostility when she became the first black president of the county PTA; and Carrie Winter, who had worked hard with Maggie Ray on the CAG; and white attorneys Ward McKeithen and Ashley Hogewood, who had seen their children bused to Billingsville Elementary, back in the days before its future was assured. Like other parents, McKeithen and Hogewood had rolled up their sleeves, and working with the blacks who were already there, they had transformed Billingsville into a model school—improving its physical plant and its tangible resources, creating a favorable climate in which any child could learn. It had not been easy, they could tell you, but it had been worth it, and the irritating thing about the Sardis Forest parents, the thing that made them seem like whiners, was that they were not even being asked to do all that. The transformation of First Ward had already occurred. It had flourished under the leadership of two strong principals, a black man named Preston Allison, who soon won the confidence of his new constituency of whites, and later, Cleo Gullick, a white woman who knew how to get the best from an outstanding faculty.

Still, First Ward had been a shock when the whites first arrived in 1970. Its neighborhood students were black and poor; its tiny, cramped campus was strewn with broken glass, and its library was awful by the standards of white schools. But the whites brought resources to attack those problems. They brought money to the PTA, and they brought political influence—and gradually First Ward began to change. Working with black parents, they began with something basic—a fence to keep their children from darting into the street—and the transformation continued from there. They negotiated with the city to expand the First Ward playground and began raising money for supplemental materials. Then, with morale on the rise, they took a hard look at the school's urban neighbors—a science museum, an arts center, an Afro-American Cultural Center, several major banks and business institutions—and they began to involve them all in the academic life of the school. The result was that First Ward became a model, the kind of school in which any parent could take a great deal of pride.

So the school board rejected the Sardis Forest protest, and did it rather curtly.

David Scheick accepted the outcome with essential good grace. His oldest child was there when First Ward opened in the fall of 1986 (his youngest had been assigned to a school close to home), and he was effusive in his praise for First Ward and its faculty. "Just super," he said. Nevertheless, Scheick was disturbed by the reception he had received from the school board, and some months later, in seeking to make sense of it, he offered a postmortem with perplexing implications: "Every year, two thousand kids are moved. This might be the single best way, but it's at least worth a study. The school system has got to have a long-range plan. We need to find out if stability is possible. The problem was, when the discussion started, if you said *one word*, if you even suggested that there *might* be some problems with the busing plan, you were immediately branded a Yankee racist pig, somebody who doesn't know or care about the history of integration. That's not true, and that has to change. There are a lot of *me*'s in Charlotte these days."

Jay Robinson knew there was some truth in that. It was indisputably true that there were a great many parents like David Scheick in Charlotte, good and decent people who were recent arrivals, and who simply had not lived through all the city's struggles. Those people were, in fact, among the central players in Robinson's greatest nightmare. It was not a nightmare that he shared with many people, and indeed he did not even like to think about it himself. But it went something like this: The external pressure continued to build, with the antibusing policies of the Reagan administration, and the occasional pronouncements of Senator Jesse Helms, the state's senior official in Washington, fueling ideological opposition in Charlotte. Obviously, that was already beginning to happen, and Robinson feared that in volatile combination with a few other ingredients, it could spell disaster for the consensus for integration. Indeed, a second ingredient was already present: the frustrations of parents such as David Scheick, who buttressed their indignation with rational-sounding arguments about long-range planning. It was not that simple, of course. Long-range planning was an ongoing process, but a rigid, immutable formula—devoid of annual tinkerings—was a contradiction in terms in a city of rapid growth and demographic change.

But all of that was very hard to explain, and in his darker moments, Robinson sometimes marveled that the consensus still held—especially since he could see the possibility of yet another ingredient, a twist of history so ironic and so depressing, and so potentially irresistible if it got out of hand, that it could achieve the critical mass he was working to resist. That critical ingredient was the frustration of blacks. The possibility was not as farfetched as it sounded, for the feeling was already present on the board of education in the person of Arthur Griffin, a young black businessman with a genuine passion for education. Griffin had grown up poor and had worked his way up from the housing projects, with education as one of his major tools. Now in his mid-thirties, he was just old enough to remember the liabilities of segregated classrooms: the second-rate facilities, hand-me-down books, and the uneven quality and training of his teachers. But he was also concerned about the liabilities of integration: the possibility that black students, being a minority in every school, were not always being taught with the same diligence as whites. Overall, the statistics did not support such a view. Between 1978 and 1985, black test scores had risen slightly faster than those of whites. Still, the news was not all good. Even at a school as fine as First Ward, black children were not making the progress they should. Their California Achievement Test scores had risen from the eighteenth to the forty-first percentile between 1980 and 1984, but in 1985, they fell again to the thirty-third. No matter how you cut it, that was disappointing.

It was true, of course, that the black children at First Ward were almost all poor; the majority of them lived in public housing, and they suffered from all the emotional and intellectual deprivations of the black underclass—that intractable defeatism of a people left behind. They represented a difficult challenge for the public schools of Charlotte, and while Jay Robinson was certain that the schools were making progress, he fretted sometimes that it was too incremental to satisfy the blacks. And then what? Arthur Griffin, in his heart, was committed to integration. But what if another leader came along with failed expectations that had given way to bitterness? What if that leader, stirring his followers with a rhetoric of black self-reliance, entered into an unholy alliance with the enemies of busing? Would that be the moment when it all came apart? Robinson did not think so, or at least he hoped not. But he knew the battle against such an outcome, or against other threats he had yet to imagine, was likely to be a long one, if indeed it ever ended.

The next question was how much energy he still had for the fight. By 1986, he was beginning to have serious back problems that occasionally put him in traction. At fifty-eight, he was no longer a young man. But if he was going to be superintendent, he simply didn't know how to do it half speed. Thus he began to consider changing jobs. He told his friends he was in no hurry. But when Dick Spangler, the former vice-chairman of the Charlotte school board, was chosen in January as the fourteenth president of the University of North Carolina, and when he offered Robinson a vice-presidency a few months later, Robinson decided to take it.

The members of the school board were not surprised by the move. They, too, had seen the symptoms of restlessness and stress. Even so, it was a little frightening, for the system was now thrust into a new situation. Its most effective advocate of desegregation was moving on—a man so admired by most segments of the community that he was able to win startlingly broad support for the things he believed. But the board members didn't panic. Led by their chairman, Carrie Winter, they simply went out and found a replacement. His name was Peter Relic, the Harvard-educated grandson of a Yugoslavian immigrant, a veteran of the education department in the Carter administration, whose views on desegregation appeared indistinguishable from those of Jay Robinson.

"I think busing for desegregation is right," he said, "and it's been right all along. To resegregate could be criminal for the individual child and wrong for society." Though that commitment remained to be tested, Relic seemed to have a sense also that the struggle to preserve integration, to build on the legacy of the Charlotte triumph, might never end: that the very fact of two races living side by side would require an ongoing vigilance against the worst that's still within us. And that difficult truth is not likely to vanish for as far into the future as it is possible to see.

Epilogue

Julius Chambers left Charlotte shortly before Jay Robinson. It was a sad occasion for him, for he had developed a deep affection for the city, having seen its apartheid give way to a more decent order. There was a civility now, not the paternalistic, Old South variety, but something of far greater substance: a feeling of simple respect, once limited to the dreams of Martin Luther King or to the prophetic imagination of Darius Swann.

Chambers still remembered his first meeting with Swann. It was 1964, and Darius and Vera, his wife, had just returned to Charlotte from the mission fields of India. There, they had lived in an integrated community of missionaries, and for the better part of a decade, had known the benefits of that liberation: People were people, and there was simply no need for the adjectives of color.

If the Swanns' lawsuit against the Charlotte-Mecklenburg schools had not quite achieved such a society in Charlotte, it had come far closer than Chambers would have guessed. It was tempting, he admitted, to stay put now and enjoy the benefits. But it was also June of 1984, four years into the presidency of Ronald Reagan, and when Chambers was offered the top staff job at the NAACP Legal Defense Fund, he felt he simply had to take it. Only two men had ever held that job, Thurgood Marshall and his brilliant successor Jack Greenberg, and Chambers was honored to continue that tradition. Even so, when Charlotte's white and black leadership assembled in August to bid him goodbye, he found himself choked with emotion. Bill Poe was there, and Judge McMillan, and Maggie Ray, and dozens of others who had played courageous roles in Charlotte's transformation. On that occasion, and many times afterward, Chambers spoke in glowing terms about the previous twenty years. There were even a few moments when his impeccable self-control showed symptoms of strain: "I have been," he said softly, "quite proud of Charlotte, and brag about it just about everywhere I go. I appreciate what changes have taken place here, structurally and otherwise, in relationships between people. I've taken time to describe the segregated situation I saw in 1964, and how those barriers have been removed and how people have been able to get along. It is, to me, very unique."

The striking thing was, many of the white postmortems were virtually the same. For example, Bill Poe—like Chambers and a wide variety of other observers ranging from antibusing leader Jane Scott to black *Swann* plaintiff James K. Polk—still saw problems: some white and black children falling through the cracks, as educators grappled with the dimensions of the change. But by the mid-eighties, there was wide agreement also with Poe's assessment of the sweeping benefits—how the ordeal of busing had come close to resolving the whole issue of race. "I guess there had to be a struggle somewhere," Poe concluded. "It was fought at a level that affected a great many people and in a very emotional way. People had their say on television, in the press, and then it went to the Supreme Court, and we got an ultimate answer. It had the effect of saying, 'well, this is just how things are going to be. . . .' It has surprised me in a way that the school case could have that much impact on almost everything in the Charlotte-Mecklenburg community. But it has really seemed to me to sort of resolve the race issue for the present time and the foreseeable future."

That assessment (and its similarity with the views of Julius Chambers) was in itself a measure of the change, for there had been a time back in the days of segregation, when there were two distinct views of what Charlotte was all about. Members of the white community, particularly the business and political leadership, had tended to be proud of the city's racial progress. They spoke enthusiastically about voluntary gestures toward the goal of integration—the removal of racial barriers in downtown restaurants, or the successful experiment at Central High School, where Gus Roberts broke the color line in 1957. That was the same year that federal troops were called in to restore peace during a desegregation crisis in Little Rock, Arkansas. Charlotte's white leaders were proud of the calm that prevailed at Central High. But in the black community, the view was different. There, leaders tended to emphasize the ordeal of Dorothy Counts, who, also in 1957, was driven out of

Harding High by petty acts of violence and the threat of something worse. They would mention the bombing of the homes of civil rights leaders, and they would point out that political and economic power was almost entirely in the hands of whites.

Twenty years later, however, Charlotte's leaders, black and white, were largely in agreement about where the city stood. Together, its citizens had built one of the nation's most respected school systems. Its racial and political climate was far superior to most. And busing had been the key to all of those changes.

If there was one person prouder of all that than Julius Chambers, it was probably Judge McMillan. As of the late 1980s, he was still a respected member of the federal bench, though he fretted sometimes over the conservative drift of the courts. But the satisfaction that he drew from the *Swann* lawsuit was the kind of thing that enlarged the very meaning of his life. He could scarcely contain his admiration for the people of Charlotte. Whatever the future might hold, they had confronted the dilemma of race perhaps more honestly, and more compassionately, than any community in America.

But why had it happened? one of his friends recently asked him, as they were returning from a long conversation at lunch. How was it, really, that things had turned out so fine?

It was the week before Easter. The wind blew warmly, and there were faint wisps of clouds drifting high in the sky. McMillan didn't answer the question right away. He thought for a minute, and then he gestured toward the grounds of First Presbyterian Church, where the grass was newly green, and the dogwoods and daffodils were blooming with the season. Finally he said: "I recently joined the choir of this church. It's been pretty interesting. We sing some songs that have notes that I can't hit. But I do hit them."

He paused and grinned at the blank stare of his friend, and then finished his parable as he moved on up the street: "I hit them," he said, "because I have to."

Index

370.19 Gaillard, Frye,
GA   1946-

        The dream long
        deferred

$19.95

DATE			
DEC 0 4 2006			

© THE BAKER & TAYLOR CO.